Long ago, in Kentucky, I, a boy, stood
By a dirt road, in first dark, and heard
The great geese hoot northward.
I could not see them, there being no moon
And the stars sparse. I heard them.
I did not know what was happening in my heart.
It was the season before the elderberry blooms,
Therefore they were going north.
The sound was passing northward.

—*Robert Penn Warren*

WILDSAM PURSUITS

Places are endlessly complex: time, geography, culture and
happenings layered with millions of stories. And often, one realizes
that a place carries a specific heritage, a definitive pursuit that
people build their lives around, a common trade or precious
resource that might set the course for generations.

For Kentucky, this pursuit is bourbon.

A big thank y'all to the writers, friends and other generous locals who offered their insight and wisdom, including Ashlie Stevens [an everlasting well of enthusiasm!], Maggie Kimberl [we bow to your expertise], incredible essayists Jason Kyle Howard and Hannah L. Drake for beautiful, complex stories about Kentucky, and Wright Thompson who lent us part of his journey with Julian Van Winkle. Thank you, Adam Morrow, for the Merton mentoring. Lora Smith and Holly Weyler McKnight, we so appreciate your connections and knowledge. Rachael Sinclair, your illustrations make this book sparkle. And a special thank you to Wendell Berry for allowing us the honor of sharing his poetry. We'll all open up a bottle and pass it 'round soon.

WILDSAM FIELD GUIDES™

Published in the United States
by Wildsam Field Guides, Austin, Texas.

ISBN 978-1-4671-9956-8

Illustrations by Rachael Sinclair

To find more field guides, please visit
www.wildsam.com

CONTENTS

Discover the people and places
that tell the story of Kentucky Bourbon Country

WELCOME

—

HIS WIFE AND BELONGINGS packed in a Volkswagen Beetle, Wendell Berry, the writer-poet-activist as a young man, drove away from New York City, headed toward his ancestral home: Henry County, Kentucky. After four years teaching at NYU, Berry felt in his bones leaving the literary locus was right—his "true path." The year was 1965 and Berry not only started to farm his family's land, but he also began an inimitable harvest of prose and poetry from its soil. Now in his 80s, he told *The New Yorker* that putting together the pieces of a farm isn't far removed from writing a novel. "If they're ordered properly on a farm, something even more miraculous than most art happens: you have sustainability." The creation of something enduring, continual seems to answer the last line of his Mad Farmer's manifesto: "Practice resurrection."

Not far from Henry County, the Trappist monk Thomas Merton, another soul containing multitudes, pondered place and purpose. A troubled young man, he converted to Catholicism while studying at Columbia University, and left the city for Kentucky, as well, to live at Bardstown's Abbey of Gethsemani. Berry wrote in the quiet of his long-legged house; Merton interrogated the cosmos and the human condition in solitude amid the lonely knobs. "Happiness," he wrote there, "is not a matter of intensity but of balance, order, rhythm and harmony." The writer Walker Percy once visited Merton, who appeared in jeans and a white T-shirt. "He fixed everybody a drink, he poured me a nice bourbon and water," recalled Percy. "Well, we were right in bourbon country, you know." True, Merton's sanctuary was surrounded by centuries-old distilleries, all part of another enduring, ordered practice seeking to transcend grain and water for something greater. The rhythm of Kentucky's seasons pushes and pulls bourbon against the oak of the barrels stacked inside the rickhouses. For years, sometimes decades, the barrels sit largely undisturbed. Whatever evaporates, they call the angel's share.

In 2006, a year soon heralding the glorious revival of Kentucky's bourbon industry, a Sunday evening tornado tore through Buffalo Trace Distillery. An act of God, an act of nature, whatever it was blew apart the walls and roof of Warehouse C, yet the barrels sat in place. Ten years later, the bourbon inside proved to be some of the best ever produced there. Once, in front of a piece of art, Merton beheld "cosmic, rich, full-bodied honest victories." Maybe this was a similar triumph. Or maybe a resurrection. —The Editors

ESSENTIALS

*Trusted intel and travel info about iconic culture,
geography and entry points to the traditions and landscapes
of Kentucky Bourbon Country*

PLANNING

BIKES
Parkside Bikes
Louisville
parksidebikes.com

....

HORSEBACK RIDING
Deer Run Stables
Richmond
*@deerrunstable_*

....

CUMBERLAND FALLS
Corbin
Nicknamed "Little Niagara." One of two places in the world to see a moonbow year round.

....

JOHN A. ROEBLING BRIDGE
Covington
Brooklyn Bridge prototype was longest suspension in the world.

MAGAZINE
Louisville
Monthly pairs deep cultural reporting with powerful visuals.

....

BIZ JOURNAL
The Bourbon Review
Bottle reviews, interviews, best bourbon bars list.

....

RADIO
WFPK 91.9 FM
One of nation's best indie stations.

Central Kentucky's not-too-north and not-too-south position unveils four distinct seasons, each with its own gifts. Most anticipated are spring's magnolias, weeping cherries and dogwoods blooming in an ombre of pinks, and autumn's hardwood forests exploding in crimsons and golds. Although hot and humid, summers produce bushels of blackberries and tomatoes and fields of sunflowers [hardiness zone 6 gives a long growing season]. Winters can be icy and bone-chilling, but that's what bourbon and fireplaces are for.

JAN	Beginning of spring distillation season
FEB	National Farm Machinery Show
MAR	Southern Kentucky Book Fest
APR	Foaling season
MAY	Kentucky Derby
JUN	ROMP Bluegrass Festival
JUL	Forecastle Festival
AUG	Railbird Festival
SEP	Marion County Country Ham Days
OCT	Keeneland Fall Meet
NOV	Louisville Bourbon Classic
DEC	Anniversary of Repeal Day

GEOGRAPHY

Notable terrain formations and where to find them.

KNOB

A rounded, isolated hill or mountain. Some have capstones that form cliffs, making for adventuresome lookouts to hike toward. *Pilot Knob*

....

GORGE

A water-worn valley. The Red River formed Kentucky's own version of the Grand Canyon. *Red River Gorge*

KARST

Area of soluble rock, like limestone, wears away from the top to reveal sinkholes and underground streams. *Daniel Boone National Forest*

....

CAVE

Minerals dissolve and drain from underground rock, creating tunnels and cavernous pockets. *Mammoth Cave*

COALFIELD

Expanse containing a significant number of subterranean coal deposits. Eastern Kentucky Coalfield covers 30 counties. *Portal 31 Coal Mine*

....

NATURAL ARCH

Bridge-like rock formation, typically the result of erosion from weathering or rivers. *Natural Bridge State Park*

TRADITIONS

Beyond bourbon, a heritage of farming, food, music and sport.

Horses   A combination of rolling fields for grazing and looser 19th-century regulations for gambling created the state's now $6.5-billion industry. *Kentucky Horse Park, Lexington*

Bluegrass   Acoustic music genre combining old-time, blues and fiddle derives name from Bill Monroe and His Bluegrass Boys. *Bluegrass Music Hall of Fame & Museum, Owensboro*

Country Ham   Kentucky anchors the U.S. ham belt. Flavor cultivated from field to curehouse. *Broadbent Hams, Kuttawa*

Cooperage   Kentucky is still a major producer of the white-oak barrels used for spirit and wine aging within the state and around the world. *Kentucky Cooperage, Lebanon*

Basketball   Bragging rights remain with the UK Wildcats, Division 1's winningest college team. *Rupp Arena, Lexington*

BOURBON DESTINATIONS

A quick guide to noted distilleries, old and new, urban and rural.

BUFFALO TRACE
Established 1775. Source for many of bourbon's best names.

FOUR ROSES
Storied name made glorious return to U.S. shelves in 2002.

HARTFIELD & COMPANY
First distillery in Bourbon County post-Prohibition.

STITZEL-WELLER
A long-shuttered legend revived for Blade and Bow.

WILD TURKEY
Home to longest-tenured master distiller, Jimmy Russell.

WILLETT
Brand's Pot Still Resereve bottle echoes shape of its copper stills.

KENTUCKY PEERLESS
Founder's great-grandson revived brand in downtown Louisville.

HEAVEN HILL
Sprawling complex, the largest independently owned distillery.

JIM BEAM
Overseeen by seven generations. Booker's Bourbon an ode to one.

MAKER'S MARK
Red-shuttered black stillhouse a Bourbon Trail landmark.

CULTURAL INSTITUTIONS

MUHAMMAD ALI CENTER
144 N 6th St, Louisville

Dedicated to the life and legacy of "The Greatest." Hosts eponymous Humanitarian Awards [Dave Eggers and Jimmy Carter past winners].

....

BEREA COLLEGE
101 Chestnut St, Berea

Tuition-free liberal arts college for low-income students. Home to bell hooks Institute and several progressive initiatives focused on Appalachian culture.

....

BLUEGRASS MUSIC HALL OF FAME & MUSEUM
311 W 2nd St, Owensboro

Half an hour from the preserved home of Bill Monroe, father of bluegrass. Traces the form's roots and place in American music canon.

SCENIC DRIVES AND PUBLIC LANDS

Back roads and natural sites throughout the heart of Kentucky.

KENTUCKY RIVER PALISADES

The Kentucky River cuts a jade path through sheer limestone bluffs. Paddlers, turn off at the High Bridge on the short but stunning Dix River, where trout swim below and eagles swoop above. *Shakertown*

....

OLD FRANKFORT PIKE

Unofficially known as "Thoroughbred Alley." Two-laner rolls by horse-flocked fields and quilt-starred barns hemmed in by fences of slate-painted wood or dry-laid stacked rocks. *Frankfort to Lexington*

....

RED RIVER GORGE

A canyon that contains multitudes within its nearly 30,000 acres. More than 100 sandstone arches and waterfalls with expectation-setting names [i.e., Creation Falls]. Paradise for rock climbers. *Slade*

....

BERNHEIM ARBORETUM AND RESEARCH FOREST

Don't be startled by Mama Loumari, Little Nis and Little Elina. These three fantastical wooden creatures sleep under the trees along the Forest Giants Trail. The canopy walk 75 feet above provides a perfect perch to view the cascade of fall color from the top down. *Shepherdsville*

....

DANIEL BOONE NATIONAL FOREST

Reaching across 21 counties, the protected forest also covers Cumberland Falls and the Sheltowee Trace Trail, where a skinny footbridge fit for Indiana Jones hangs over Jump Rock, an equally cinematic monolith rising from the Red River. *Corbin*

....

U.S. 23 COUNTRY MUSIC HIGHWAY

A scooch east from Central Kentucky. Dwight Yoakam, Chris Stapleton and Tom T. Hall all hail from this stretch. It also passes by Loretta Lynn's childhood home in Butcher Holler. *Ashland to Pikeville*

....

DUNCAN HINES SCENIC BYWAY

Commemorates the food critic, cake-mix namesake and son of Bowling Green. Green River ferry ride too. *Bowling Green*

CULTURE

FILM

Elizabethtown

Stripes

Coal Miner's Daughter

*Look & See: A Portrait
of Wendell Berry*

Rain Man

hillbilly

Goldfinger

Seabiscuit

Harlan County, USA

Trumbo

The Insider

MUSIC

Tom T. Hall
Storyteller, Poet, Philosopher

Loretta Lynn
Van Lear Rose

John Prine
"Paradise"

Bill Monroe
and His Blue Grass Boys
"Kentucky Waltz"

My Morning Jacket
It Still Moves

BOOKS

↦ *The Art of Loading Brush* by Wendell Berry: A more recent collection by the poet, author, small-farm visionary, rural champion and, most importantly, Henry County resident. Berry's agrarian ethos remains relevant in a mix of real-world essays and fictional tales from Port William.

....

↦ *Clay's Quilt* by Silas House: Appalachian folkways from fiddling to quilting weave through a story of how an orphan finds a chosen family.

....

↦ *Bright Dead Things* by Ada Limón: Lexington transplant by way of Sonoma, California. With poems like the Pushcart-winning "How to Triumph Like a Girl," this collection ruminates on her new Kentucky home.

....

↦ *All the Living* by C.E. Morgan: Debut novel from Berea College alumna turned Pulitzer finalist. A tobacco farm sets the scene for a classic yet complicated love story made fresh and bracing by Morgan's local perspective.

....

↦ *Blood Horses: Notes of a Sportswriter's Son* by John Jeremiah Sullivan: Sullivan sees his father in a new light by way of the human-horse connection.

....

↦ *Perfect Black* by Crystal Wilkinson: Kentucky's poet laureate explores her intersecting identities as a Black woman born of Appalachia.

ISSUES

Police Conduct	Kentucky, and the entire country, are still reeling from the police shooting of Breonna Taylor, a 26-year-old Black EMT. While some progress has been made [Louisville recently banned no-knock warrants like the one that led to Taylor's death, for instance] people of color are still disproportionately arrested for low-level offenses, searched in traffic stops and overrepresented in the state prison population. **EXPERT:** *Attica Scott, Kentucky State Representative*
Post-Coal Economy	More than 10,000 coal workers have been laid off since 2008, many in areas already grappling with cyclical poverty. Some are turning to burgeoning industries like renewables, coding and hydroponic farming as possible solutions. **EXPERT:** *Colby Hall, executive director, SOAR*
Warming Summers	It's unclear how exactly hotter temps from climate change could impact the bourbon aging process. One possibility: more liquid might be lost during evaporation in non-climate-controlled rickhouses. **EXPERT:** *Dr. Lindell Ormsbee, University of Kentucky*
Barrel Taxes	While Kentucky remains in the midst of a sustained bourbon boom, it's still the only place in the world that taxes aging barrels of spirits, which industry members say puts state distillers at a competitive disadvantage. **EXPERT:** *Eric Gregory, president, Kentucky Distillers' Association*

STATISTICS

1.1 million..Acres of land devoted to horses
600 ....Potential unexplored miles within Mammoth Cave
$8.6 billion ....Value of Kentucky's bourbon industry
48 ......Blocks in Old Louisville, largest Victorian home collection in U.S.
92,000 .... Barrels lost to 1996 fire at Heaven Hill Distillery
859 ....Waterfalls in the state

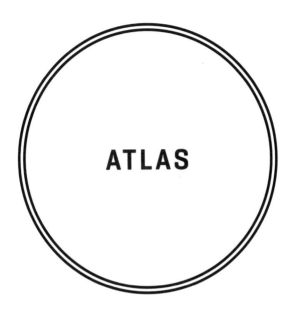

ATLAS

———

A guide to the lands and places of Kentucky Bourbon Country, including curated favorites, communities large and small, and a road trip from the city to the countryside

BESTS

FOOD & DRINK

ALL-DAY

The Grales

1001 Baxter Ave Louisville

Highlands house a longtime favorite for biscuit sandwiches, rye cookies. Chapel turned beer bar across twinkly courtyard.

....

KENTUCKY CLASSICS

Wallace Station

3854 KY Route 1681 Versailles

Ouita Michel's Bourbon Trail pit stop known for inside-out hot browns.

....

SUSHI

School

163 W Short St Lexington

Best for nigiri, hand rolls among Kentucky's collection of Japanese restaurants.

COCKTAILS

ONA

108 Church St Lexington

In one local's words, a "sexy terrarium" for cheeky, seasonally minded concoctions and a primo natural wine selection.

....

BOURBON BAR

The Silver Dollar

1761 Frankfort Ave Louisville

Bakersfield Sound-inspired honky-tonk in Butchertown also has single-barrel flights.

....

Talbott Tavern

107 W Stephen Foster Bardstown

Oldest bourbon bar in the country. Stone walls and big timber beams, circa 1779.

SOUTHERN-ITALIAN

bar Vetti

727 E Market St Louisville

Saucy NuLu spot makes chicken parm seem glam. Country sausage on the pizza, dried-apple dressing on the Casesar.

....

DELI & BOOZE

Morris Deli

2228 Taylorsville Rd Louisville

Liquor store lunch counter serves a mean country ham salad sandwich.

....

GLOBAL SOUTHERN

610 Magnolia

610 W Magnolia Ave Louisville

Edward Lee's tasting menus still a cornerstone of Louisville's restaurant scene.

CUBAN

Mi Sueño
3425 Bardstown Rd
Louisville
U.S.' third-largest Cuban community calls city home. Ropa vieja, rice, mango juice.

....

CAFETERIA

Keeneland Track Kitchen
4201 Versailles Rd
Lexington
Buffet line with big street cred from locals and jockeys.

....

SOUL FOOD

Shirley Mae's Cafe
802 S Clay St
Louisville
Cash only. From scratch. Blackberry cobbler mandatory.

....

COFFEE & COOKIE

Please & Thank You
800 E Market St
Louisville
Neighborhood vinyl and coffee shop also a cookie empire.

....

CLASSIC

Dudley's on Short
259 W Short St
Lexington
Locally sourcing since 1981.

LAID-BACK LOUNGE

meta
425 W Chestnut St
Louisville
Copper-penny-tiled lounge for serious cocktails minus the pretense.

....

PIZZA

Miguel's
1890 Natural Bridge Rd
Slade
Climbing gear shop and wood-fired pies by Red River Gorge.

....

BURGERS

Laha's Red Castle
21 Lincoln Square
Hodgenville
Flat top smash patties since 1934.

....

DOUGHNUTS

Spalding's Bakery
760 Winchester Rd
Lexington
Hand rolled since 1929. Go straight-up glazed or apple fritter.

....

DINER

Ferrell's Snappy Services
1001 S Main St
Hopkinsville
Retro neon. Checkered paper-lined baskets. Chili bowls.

BAKERY

Wiltshire Pantry
901 Barret Ave
Louisville
Fork-scored tarts, sourdough loaves, sweet potato melts, plus coffee.

....

LOCAL CUTS

Marksbury Farm Market
7907 Nicholasville Rd
Lancaster
Farm restaurant serves its own pastured animals.

....

MEXICAN

Tortillería Y Taquería Ramírez
1429 Alexandria Dr
Lexington
Mainstay of "Mexington."

....

PIES

Magee's Baking Co.
414 Market Square Dr
Maysville
Famous for transparent pie. Counts Clooney as a fan.

....

BURGOO

Dave's Sticky Pig
106 Madison Square Dr
Madisonville
Barbecue shack makes a mean stew.

LODGING

ART-FOCUSED
21C Museum Hotel
Louisville
museumhotels.com
Flagship of the contemporary art-driven chain. 9,000 square feet of galleries. Red penguins.

....

STORIED STAY
The Brown Hotel
Louisville
brownhotel.com
Ornate-as-all-get-out lobby with marble, mahogany and hand-painted ceilings.

....

FARM B&B
Eighth Pole Inn
Lexington
eighthpoleinn.com
Spruced-up suites on a working horse farm.

....

SMALL-TOWN SUITE
Boone Tavern
Berea
boonetavernhotel.com
Owned by Berea College. Partially built by students in 1909.

HISTORIC HOTEL
The Seelbach Hilton
Louisville
seelbachhilton.com
If the guilded staircase looks like Jay Gatsby is about to descend, there's a reason why.

....

ON THE RIVER
Hotel Covington
Covington
hotelcovington.com
A hop across the Ohio from Cincinnati. Modern remodel of state's first skyscraper.

....

CONTEMPORARY CASTLE
The Kentucky Castle
Versailles
thekentuckycastle.com
On-property amenities from apiary to cryotherapy chamber.

....

NEW IN TOWN
The Grady
Louisville
thegradyhotel.com
River-view rooms. Once a medicinal bourbon apothecary.

HORSE COUNTRY
The Campbell House
Lexington
thecampbellhouse.com
Ivory barn buildings with clubhouse-style rooms and fireplace-warmed lobby. Close to Keeneland.

....

NATURE RETREAT
DuPont Lodge
Corbin
parks.ky.gov
State park-run lodge on Cumberland Falls. Observation deck. Fire tower.

....

TREE HOUSE
Canopy Crew
Red River Gorge
thecanopycrew.com
Tiny houses perched over cliffs, arches. Stargaze from bed.

....

COTTAGE STAY
Stanford Inn
Stanford
wildernessroadguest.com
Small-town guesthouses with farm-focused cafe and spa.

OUTDOORS

STABLE TOUR

Horse Country

Lexington

visithorsecountry.com

More than 30 different options: behind the scenes at Keeneland, private farms, even feed-makers.

....

PARK SYSTEM

The Parklands of Floyds Fork

Louisville

theparklands.org

A 4,000-acre system. Olmsted's legacy envisioned for the future.

....

FORAGING GUIDE

The Hungry Forager

Louisville

thehungryforager.com

George Barnett leads immersive walks for finding wild food.

....

AERIAL VIEW

Natural Bridge Skylift

Slade

naturalbridgeskylift andgiftshop.com

Ride through Red River Gorge canopy.

PRESIDENTIAL ORIGINS

Abraham Lincoln Birthplace

Hodgenville

nps.gov

Home to first, smaller memorial. Replica of one-room cabin where he was born.

....

CAVE PADDLE

SUP Kentucky

Rogers

supkentucky.com

Paddle through neon-lit caverns and limestone tunnels in Lucite-clear kayaks.

....

BOTANICA

State Botanical Garden of Kentucky

Lexington

arboretum.ca.uky.edu

Low-impact way to behold autumn color.

....

JAPANESE GARDEN

Yuko-en Garden

Georgetown

yukoen.com

Tokugawa gates lead to bluegrass and cherry blossoms.

FARM

Hermitage Farm

Goshen

hermitagefarm.com

21c Museum Hotel owners' new bucolic project. Horses, art, bourbon, dazzling dinners.

....

HISTORIC PARK

Shaker Village

Harrodsburg

shakervillageky.org

Guest rooms, farm, restaurant, shop revolve around Shaker craft and culture.

....

WATERFALL

Pine Island Double Falls

London

Twin waterfalls wed their spills at the end of a tricky trail.

....

ARCHITECTURE WALK

Old Louisville

Louisville

U.S.' largest assemblage of Victorian architecture and homes with stained glass.

SHOPS

LIQUOR STORE
Toddy's
110 S 4th St
Bardstown
Guthrie McKay's
unassuming quickie
mart lit by neon beer
signs has hard-to-find,
top-shelf bourbons.

....

FLOWERS
Brownings Farm &
Flower Truck
@brownings
flowertruck
Coast guard vet
Lauren Spencer rolls
her perfectly patinaed
baby-blue truck
around Cynthiana.

....

RECORDS
Guestroom Records
1806 Frankfort Ave
Louisville
Crates of new and
used. Indie zines too.

....

BUTCHER CASE
Red Hog
2622 Frankfort Ave
Louisville
Whole-animal ethos.
Charcuterie boards.

STATE PRIDE
Kentucky for
Kentucky
720 Bryan Ave
Lexington
The brand behind
those blue-and-white
"Y'ALL" shirts you've
seen. Learn the legend
of Cocaine Bear.

....

COUNTRY STORE
Penn's Store
257 Penn's Store Rd
Gravel Switch
Looks just about like
it did when the Penns
took over in 1850.

....

VINTAGE
The Nitty Gritty
996 Barret Ave
Louisville
Splashy formal-wear
section for offbeat
Derby duds.

....

LEATHER AND GLASS
Clayton & Crume
216 S Shelby St
Louisville
All manner of mono-
grammable items,
like rocks glasses.

OUTFITTER
J&H Lanmark
189 Moore Dr
Lexington
Indie outdoors shop
a staple for area's rock
climbers, paddlers and
hikers. Solid advice
for first-time gorge or
forest explorers.

....

HATS
Formé Millinery
1009 E Main St,
Louisville
Owner Jenny
Pfanenstiel a master
couture-level hatter.

....

MARKET
Logan Street Market
1001 Logan St
Louisville
Year-round indoor
farmers market.
Bagel counter. Bar.

....

BOOKSTORES
Poor Richard's Books
Frankfort
Carmichael's
Louisville
Joseph-Beth
Lexington

BOURBON HISTORY

Frazier Kentucky History Museum
Louisville
fraziermuseum.org
Smithsonian affiliate has modern interpretation of state's history. Official Bourbon Trail start point.

....

INTERIOR DESIGN

Bittners Inc.
Louisville
bittners.com
Contemporary yet classic firm started as 1854 cabinet shop.

....

CONCERT

Louisville Orchestra
Louisville
louisvilleorchestra.org
Led by conductor Teddy Abrams, who rides bike to concerts, eschews tuxedos.

....

WRITING

Carnegie Center
Lexington
carnegiecenter.org
Workshops, deep discussions, poetry.

COPPER STILLS

Vendome Copper & Brass Works
Louisville
vendomecopper.com
Fourth generation metal fabricator famous for copper stills used by many bourbon distillers.

....

DULCIMERS

Warren A. May
Berea
warrenamay.com
Carves the best examples of the traditional fretted instrument.

....

LETTERPRESS

Larkspur Press
Monterey
larkspurpress.com
Handset type and handmade paper.

....

DANCE FLOOR

Omega National Products
Louisville
omeganational products.com
Country's top disco ball manufacturer.

APPALACHIAN CRAFT

Log House Craft Gallery
Berea
bcloghousecrafts.com
Berea College purveyor and preserver of all things hand-hewn. Baskets, brooms, blankets and bowls.

....

BRANDY

Copper & Kings
Louisville
copperandkings.com
No bourbon, but still acclaimed. Absinthe, bitters, gin too.

....

BASEBALL

Louisville Slugger Museum & Factory
Louisville
sluggermuseum.com
Weapon of choice for the greats. Made here since 1884.

....

COUNTRY HAM

Nancy Mahaffey
newsomscountry ham.com
Learned art of aging from her father.

EVENTS

BIKE COMPETITION

Bourbon
Country Burn

Lexington
@bourboncountryburn

Three-day, 250-mile
bicycle tour to 11
distilleries. Many
dedicated return
cyclists camp out on
the ride too.

....

CAR SHOW

Somernites Cruise

Somerset
somernitescruise.com

Quarterly car show
brings in a parade of
classics.

....

JUG MUSIC

National Jug Band
Jubilee

Louisville
@ jugbandjubilee

Annual gathering in
the home city of the
old-time genre.

....

TRAIL RUN

Bluegrass Cup

@bluegrasscup

Trail race [5K and
10K] through forest.

HORSE RACE

Kentucky Derby

Louisville
kentuckyderby.com

Two-minute race pre-
ceded by a monthlong
festival. Elegance and
debauchery on full
display from infield to
Millionaires' Row.

....

BOURBON FESTIVAL

Bourbon Classic

Louisville
bourbonclassic.com

Master distillers,
renowned bartenders
and chefs convene.

....

SHEEP SHOW

Kentucky Sheep and
Fiber Festival

Lexington
@kentuckysheepand
fiberfestival

Wool and yarn
enthusiasts unite.

....

FOOD FESTIVAL

Beer Cheese Festival

Winchester
beercheesefestival.com

Fierce competition.
Soft pretzels.

DESTINATION FESTIVAL

Forecastle Festival

Louisville
forecastlefest.com

Three days of big-
time touring acts
on the Ohio River.
Bourbon tent. Activ-
ism arm too.

....

CHRISTMAS

Hillenmeyer
Christmas Shop

Lexington
@hillenmeyerchristmas

Astonishingly idyllic
winter wonderland.
Trees, wreaths, cider,
marshmallow roasts.

....

DISTILLING EDUCATION

Moonshine
University

Louisville
@Moonshine_U

Spirited workshops
and six-week courses.

....

TREASURE HUNT

127 Yard Sale

127yardsale.com

"The world's longest
yard sale" along
Highway 127.

EXPERTS

HOSPITALITY

Ed Lee & Lindsey
Ofcacek
The Lee Initiative
Chef-driven
nonprofit aims to
solve long-standing
issues in hospitality
industry, from equity
to training.

....

ICE CLIMBING

Mike Wilkinson
@wilkinsonvisual
Documentary maker
chases and scales
Kentucky's fleeting
frozen falls.

....

BOURBON WRITER

Fred Minnick
@FredMinnick
Author, journalist
and podcast host
talks brown water
with guests like Killer
Mike and Daryl Hall.

....

PARKS

Layla George
olmstedparks.org
Head of Louisville's
Olmsted Parks
Conservancy.

BOURBON TRAIL TOUR

Kaitlyn Soligan &
Nicole Stipp
Matson & Gilman
Refreshingly reimag-
ined guide company
custom builds trips to
distilleries, bars, etc.

....

APPALACHIAN FOOD

Ronni Lundy
@ronnilundy
Corbin-born cookbook
author's acclaimed
Victuals contextualizes
recipes like soup beans
and stack cakes.

....

PROGRESSIVE FARMING

Sam Halcomb
walnutgrovefarms.com
Grows grains used
in bourbon distilling
on 18th-century
transitioned farm.

....

MEMES

Kenneth Pergram
@littlebubbychild
Instagram's unlikely
sensation. Hilarious,
endearing characters.
Ye mamaws, hosscats
and cousins.

GARDEN DESIGN

Jon Carloftis
@JonCarloftis
One of the South-
east's best landscape
minds. Sculpted
grounds of Maker's
Mark and Castle &
Key distilleries.

....

POETRY

Crystal Wilkinson
crystalewilkinson.net
Kentucky's poet
laureate also a key
contemporary
figure in the state's
Affrilachian poetry
tradition.

....

IMPACT INVESTMENT

Lora Smith
@LoraEliSmith
Food writer also
leads efforts to
fund state's next
economic chapter.

....

LOCAL HISTORY

Tom Owen
louisville.edu
Leads city history
tours on bicycle and
YouTube channel.

CITIES & TOWNS

Legacy-rich metros, midsize cities on the come-up and bucolic small towns dot Kentucky's center. Here, ten communities to drink in.

LOUISVILLE

All eyes are on Louisville for "the most exciting two minutes in sports" every year. But for the past decade, entrepreneurs and creatives have been betting on the city, and the wager has paid off. The 30-foot-tall gold statue of Michaelangelo's *David* stands outside one of the early gambles, the first 21C MUSEUM HOTEL [now one of 11 nationwide properties]. The NuLu neighborhood isn't so new anymore, but hip Italian spot BAR VETTI is a welcome addition, while pizza at GARAGE BAR remains a favorite. Brandy and liqueur distiller Copper & Kings anchors Butchertown, and the SPEED ART MUSEUM has brought artists from Warhol to Ai Weiwei since a silvery 2016 renovation. The city's next transformation: a much-anticipated expansion of Waterfront Park will connect downtown and the city's west side.

SHOW STOP	POPULATION: 617,638
Zanzabar	COFFEE: Sunergos Coffee
Breakout acts, glitter totchos and pinball wizards	BEST DAY OF THE YEAR: Kentucky Derby, First Saturday in May

LEXINGTON

From the city's eastside "Mexington" neighborhood to its now well-established Japanese restaurants and a new generation of internationally influenced chefs, the Horse Capital of the World grew one of the country's most fascinating food scenes while everyone was busy watching the ponies. TORTILLERÍA Y TAQUERÍA RAMÍREZ makes all their tortillas, now local classics, by hand. SAV'S serves West African standards and ice cream. And Tachibana, a byproduct of the decades-old Toyota plant nearby, has noodles, katsu and sushi [as does School downtown]. At HONEYWOOD, Lawrence Weeks hosts pop-ups, like Sam Fore's Tuk Tuk Sri Lankan Bites, and at Atomic Ramen, Dan Wu crafts comforting bowls in between Lexington boosterism on his WUKY 91.3 FM podcast *Advanced D&D.*

SCOOP STOP	POPULATION: 322,570
Crank & Boom	COFFEE: Broomwagon Bikes + Cafe
Scoops like blackberry and buttermilk or bourbon and honey	BEST DAY OF THE YEAR: Railbird Festival, August

BARDSTOWN

Originally settled in 1780, Bardstown's downtown district holds nearly 200 buildings on the National Register of Historic Places. Stay in the brick-paved heart at the TALBOTT INN, an old stagecoach stop turned plush B&B with a heck of a guestbook: exiled King Louis Philippe of France, Abraham Lincoln, John James Audubon and outlaw Jesse James. Come September, the otherwise sleepy OSCAR GETZ WHISKEY MUSEUM sees an uptick in tipsy tourists and spirits professionals for the annual Kentucky Bourbon Festival, which includes a vintage bottle auction. Drive southward through the knobs toward ABBEY OF GETHSEMANI, where unorthodox religious scholar Thomas Merton lived and wrote, and an order of Trappist monks still sells honey, fruitcake and strawberry preserves reaped from its rustic property.

TRAIL STOP	POPULATION: 13,567
Elm Lick Trail	COFFEE: Fresh Coffee, Pastries & More
5-mile hike through grasslands,	BEST DAY OF THE YEAR:
valleys and beech forests	Kentucky Bourbon Festival, September

FRANKFORT

The capital city sits astride a twisty S in the Kentucky River. Early risers can watch the heavy blanket of fog lift from its double curve with a cup of coffee and warm, buttered cornbread at CLIFFSIDE DINER. Head down to the water and book a boat tour with KENTUCKY RIVER CRUISES to connect with the port town's history [and sneak a look at Buffalo Trace Distillery]. Serious trail runners, hit waterfall-pocketed COVE SPRING PARK; those seeking a less bumpy afternoon, meander through the downtown district, unexpectedly abundant with sculpture and murals [more than 10,0000 plants compose the courthouse's floral clock] or stroll into REBECCA RUTH CANDY factory, which has been sending Kentucky cream pull candy and bourbon balls down the conveyor belt since 1919. At sunset, grab a sidewalk table at SERAFINI, a bustling bistro overlooking the capitol grounds. The order: bison meatloaf.

BOOK STOP	POPULATION: 28,602
Poor Richard's Books	COFFEE: Kentucky Coffeetree Cafe
Specializes in Kentucky	BEST DAY OF THE YEAR:
and regional authors	Kentucky River Jam & Music Fest,
	monthly through the summer

OWENSBORO

During the mid-19th century, an influx of Scottish farmers who settled in the heartland of Kentucky started sheep farming and producing lambs at record-setting rates. As time marched on, a mix of immigrant ingenuity and Southern flavors melded to become a local staple: barbecued mutton. That tradition is carried on at the famed MOONLITE BAR-B-Q, which serves over 10,000 pounds of hickory-smoked and vinegar-mopped mutton a week. Each May, the city hosts the International Bar-B-Q Festival, a celebration of slow-roasted meats, burgoo stew and square dancing. The BLUEGRASS MUSIC HALL OF FAME & MUSEUM chronicles the genre's development, from its early ties to American Gospel to modern-day branches like jam grass and new grass, through interactive exhibitions and their annual festival, ROMP.

SHOP STOP	POPULATION: 60,183
Owensboro Trading Post	COFFEE: The Creme Coffee House
Sprawling antique shop	BEST DAY OF THE YEAR:
packed with unusual finds	Daylilies bloom, June

COVINGTON

In 1946, Robert Glier returned to Covington after fighting in World War II and immediately purchased a small storefront with a kitchen. He set about making goetta [pronounced GET-uh], a German-inspired breakfast sausage made with seasoned pork, beef and steel-cut oats. To this day, Glier's Meats is still family-run, and its goetta is a local staple, served alongside eggs, on pizza and—in the case of the City Goat Tavern's Goetta Hanky Panky appetizer— atop rye bread with cheese. The influence of the German immigrants who flooded Covington over the 19th century is apparent beyond the table. In the 1970s, officials created the MAINSTRASSE VILLAGE, a walkable historic district intended to protect the city's timbered German village-style architecture. Take a break from the brown water for a steiner at low-key haunts like BOURBON HAUS 1841 and Mainstrasse Village Pub.

BAKERY STOP	POPULATION: 40,181
Chako Bakery Cafe	COFFEE: The Roost Latonia
Japanese bakery with pillowy milk	BEST DAY OF THE YEAR:
bread and matcha roll cake	Goettafest, August

PARIS

Founded around 1775, Paris was called Bourbonton originally, in appreciation of the French for their aid during the American Revolution, before it was renamed in 1815. Over two centuries later, city officials doubled down on the transatlantic reference and installed a 20-foot replica of the EIFFEL TOWER in the city center. It sits adjacent to PARADISE CAFE, a quaint Vietnamese restaurant and inn where owner Lee Nguyen is known for bún bò beef and noodle soup. In the vein of sites that feel distinctly Kentucky, there's CLAIBORNE FARM—where the legendary Secretariat is buried—and COLVILLE COVERED BRIDGE. At one time, the state had 400 covered bridges; today, only 13 remain. Pass through on your way to The Bourbon Drive-In for a movie under the stars. Locals support the concession stand but know to pack a flask to augment the soft drinks.

DRINK STOP	POPULATION: 10,171
Reed Valley Orchard	COFFEE: Lil's Coffee House
Autumnal quencher:	BEST DAY OF THE YEAR:
an apple cider slushie	Paris Storytelling Festival, October

VERSAILLES

Versailles [pronounced ver-SAYLZ] is peak Kentucky horse country: miles of rolling bluegrass fields dotted by stables, latticed by sturdy black wooden fences. The BLUEGRASS SCENIC RAILROAD propels you through rows of soybeans, tobacco and two thoroughbred horse farms before descending into rugged limestone cuts. Disembark quickly—the line for country ham and pimento cheese sandwiches forms early at Chef Ouita Michel's WALLACE STATION. Not far, ECKERT'S ORCHARD offers a pick-your-own grove and WILDSIDE WINERY, an abandoned cattle farm turned vineyard, pours a bourbon barrel-aged Cabernet Sauvignon. Get *The Crown* season three vibes in the circular drive of The Kentucky Castle, an opulent B&B, surprisingly built in 1969.

DIVE STOP	POPULATION: 10,347
Wilson's Pool Room	COFFEE: The Amsden
Throw down a rack with cold	BEST DAY OF THE YEAR:
beer, diner-style burgers	Woodford County Fair and
	Saddlebred Show, July

HOPKINSVILLE

Origin point of the extraterrestrial idiom "little green men" and major producer of at-home baking mixes [hence, the nickname Battertown, U.S.A.], Hopkinsville has no shortage of colorful, curious history. Former residents include feminist author bell hooks; America's "Sleeping Prophet," Edgar Cayce; groundbreaking Black journalist Ted Poston; and Gant Gaither, Broadway's youngest producer in his day as well as Grace Kelly confidant. [Locals sometimes sport his Zoophisticates silk scarfs.] Downtown isn't scant on unexpected charms either, from the blinking marquee of the ALHAMABRA THEATRE to Saturday morning's farmers market and HOPKINSVILLE BREWING CO.'s taproom and patio. One more surprise? Get SCUBA certified just a mile and a half from the brewery at PENNYROYAL SCUBA CENTER, a blue-water, spring-fed rock quarry.

HISTORY STOP	POPULATION: 31,180
Trail Of Tears Pow Wow	COFFEE: The Corner Coffeehouse
Annual gathering remembers Native	BEST DAY OF THE YEAR:
ancestors' time in this land	Hoptown Half Marathon
	& 5K, September

CORBIN

Many end up in Corbin out of roadside-attraction curiosity to see where Colonel Harland Sanders started serving fried chicken from SANDERS COURT & CAFE, which Kentucky-born food critic Duncan Hines called "a very good place to stop en route to Cumberland Falls and the Great Smokies" in his 1939 guide. It turns out fried chicken is still a good way to fuel up before a hike or a paddle to the impressive Niagara-like falls. But the sandwich version at THE WRIGLEY TAPROOM & EATERY, with sorghum hot honey and housemade pickles, is a big improvement. If you hit town on a trifecta of a rushing river, full moon and cloudless night, head to the CUMBERLAND FALLS STATE RESORT PARK upper outlook to see a wildly rare moonbow, a prism formed by lunar light shining through the waterfall's mist.

NATURE STOP	POPULATION: 7,856
Laurel River Lake	COFFEE: You and Me
Sandy beaches, clear azure water,	Coffee and Tea
shoreline swims and fishing	BEST DAY OF THE YEAR:
	Moonbow Eggfest, September

ROAD TRIP

Criss-cross the heart of Kentucky from the city into the country for a journey of greenspaces, horse farms, art, music and awe-inspiring caves.

LOUISVILLE GREEN SPACES

DAY 1

Follow an emerald ribbon of parks lacing through Louisville, designed by the father of American landscape architecture.

Known best as the architect of New York City's Central Park, Frederick Law Olmsted was contracted by Louisville commissioners at the same time he was designing for the Vanderbilts' palatial Biltmore estate in Asheville, NC, and the first world's fair in Chicago. His contribution to Louisville was perhaps grander: 18 parks connected by six parkways. Four of these are the last Olmsted ever designed. After his death in 1903, his sons carried out his egalitarian vision—one where all people could experience how "the enjoyment of scenery employs the mind without fatigue and yet exercises it; tranquilizes it and yet enlivens it." Although development, interstate construction, and even tornados nearly erased his plan, an ongoing grassroots revival begun in the 1970s has made Louisville a leader in park protection and rehabilitation. Below, noted green spaces from Olmsted's design.

ALGONQUIN, IROQUOIS AND CHEROKEE PARKS Olmsted originals referred to as "the big three." Today, Algonquin serves as an urban community gathering spot, with a pool and playground; Cherokee has a 2.4-mile scenic drive looping through meadows and historic homes; and Iroquois carves out a tract of wilderness once called "Louisville's own Yellowstone."

WILLOW PARK This gazeboed pocket park on Cherokee's eastern side has its own personality and plays host to a summer concert series.

SENECA PARK The last one created by the Olmsted firm. Lantern-lit paved trails [for people and horses], tennis courts and an 18-hole golf course.

CENTRAL PARK At 16 acres, it's only 2 percent of the size of Manhattan's. Olmsted's sons placed a Mediterranean-ish pergola at the center to draw passersby into its serenity.

CHICKASAW PARK Severed from the system during segregation, it is the only Olmsted firm-designed park in the U.S. once designated for Black residents only. Althea Gibson, the first Black woman to win Wimbledon, played a tournament on its clay tennis courts—still free to the public.

SHELBY PARK Vintage postcards of Shelby Park show its once-massive ring-shaped pool. Today, it's home to indoor farmers market Logan Street Market and a library branch.

DAY 2

INTO HORSE COUNTRY

Taking in all the postcard-perfect pastoral beauty is as much a spectator sport as the races.

THOROUGHBRED ALLEY Also known as Old Frankfort Pike, the verdant 16.9-mile route marks a path to the country's equine capital. Osage orange, redbud and sugar maple branches weave together overhead, forming a dense, knotty canopy that breaks every few miles to reveal bluegrass pastures unfurling across the land. These fields nurture some of the region's most competitive young racehorses. Note the names Darby Dan, Lane's End and Adena Springs as you pass more than a dozen farms lined with limestone fences.

KEENELAND RACE COURSE The historic racetrack was founded in 1936 and is the state's second-most popular track after Churchill Downs. And sure, the Downs has the Kentucky Derby [an annual event that draws, on average, 150,000 attendees]. But Keeneland has the Track Kitchen. The no-frills cafeteria primarily serves track staff and horse industry members, but it's open to the public and, among locals, it's a hidden gem for early-morning biscuits and gravy and primo people watching. "It caters to everyone who is a denizen of the racetrack environment," says Ed DeRosa, marketing director for TwinSpires.com, the Kentucky Derby and Churchill Downs' official wagering site. "And the sawmill gravy is some of the best I've ever had."

KENTUCKY HORSE PARK Just 20 minutes from Keeneland, this complex is home to the 64,000-square-foot International Museum of the Horse. Sign up for a trail ride or take a seat in the bleachers for the Parade of Breeds, a daily pageant featuring some of the farm's diverse residents, from the rare Marwari to the iconic American Quarter Horse.

OLD FRIENDS FARM Leaving the park, hook a sharp right and follow a flat stretch of country road until you see a sunshine-yellow cottage with a horseshoe-shaped sign. This retirement facility gives golden years to older race and show horses, including the very dapper Silver Charm. Old Friends' owner, Michael Blowen, tells farm visitors how enamored he remains of the 1997 Kentucky Derby and Preakness winner, whom he calls "the greatest horse in the history of the universe."

ARTS AND VANISHING CRAFTS

DAY
3

Two small towns stand as the state's major
creative hubs and preservers of uniquely
American folkways.

BEREA

Founded as a one-room cabin schoolhouse by abolitionist John G. Fee
in 1855, Berea College remains a radically inclusive, tuition-free liberal
arts school and a beacon for progressive-minded Kentuckians. Find
student-made ceramics, woodcraft, even brooms in the college's shop.
For the postgraduates, the Berea Festival of Learnshops' 300 sessions
range in practice from the hammered dulcimer to Shaker-box building to
blacksmithing to basket weaving. Many of those same instructors sell their
work at downtown's Kentucky Artisan Center.

DANVILLE

The former combination post office-courthouse downtown now serves
a new civic purpose as the Art Center of the Bluegrass, a regional arts hub
with exhibits ranging from quilts to contemporary sculpture, plus a full
slate of adult classes. August's Soul of 2nd Street Festival keeps the stories
of the city's Black business district in the present and features speakers like
Danville-born Affriliachian poet Frank X Walker.

MICRODISTILLERY DETOUR

Take the less wheel-worn path from Bourbon Country's big names to discover small upstarts building on the tradition.

The tired saying goes: you can't drink all day if you don't start in the morning. But a wiser message from the locals: a day of distillery tripping should start on a full stomach. A fine first stop: FRANK'S DONUTS in Paris, Kentucky. The strip-mall shop, which opens at 4:30 a.m., is known for decadent 64-cent devil's food doughnuts. Snag one and a to-go coffee before heading downtown to HARTFIELD & CO. In 1919, the year before the "Noble Experiment" was enacted nationwide, Bourbon County was home to 26 distilleries. Prohibition put an end to them all. Though tiny compared to the big bourbon brands—even the stills they started with hold 26 gallons compared to the typical 1,000—Hartfield & Co. is a big-time addition: the first distillery to actually produce bourbon in the drink's namesake county in almost a century. Just 20 miles southwest, JAMES E. PEPPER DISTILLERY in Lexington pays homage to a Kentucky character, Colonel James E. Pepper. In the late 19th century, this colonel introduced friends with last names like Roosevelt and Rockefeller to the Old-Fashioned cocktail—a simple mix of bourbon, sugar and water garnished with an orange peel. His family's distillery, one of the oldest in the state, was left to rust in the 1950s. But after a massive restoration effort, it now anchors one of the city's buzziest districts. Continue westward to Frankfort's CASTLE & KEY DISTILLERY, an architectural marvel also risen from ruins. Originally founded in 1887, the European castle-inspired facility was opened by one of bourbonland's legends, Colonel Edmund Haynes Taylor Jr., but eventually fell into disrepair—the surrounding 113 acres overgrown, the castle collapsed. Although the property has been carefully reconstructed and was opened to the public in 2016, its bourbon is still aging. In the meantime, Castle & Key's gin, infused with botanicals from one of the many gardens on the grounds, excites the area's best bartenders. Follow Glenns Creek Road to land in downtown Frankfort and pass by the GOOCH HOUSE, the Queen Anne-style home where bourbon ball candy was allegedly invented, now the headquarters of the Kentucky Distillers' Association. Sop up the afternoon's drinking with a hearty slice of Rick's Famous Crawfish Pie on a coral Fiestaware plate at RICK'S WHITE LIGHT DINER, a charming-as-all-get-out Kentucky-Cajun greasy spoon. Ignore better judgment and finish with a slice of bourbon pecan pie, then tack a pin in your hometown on the paper map by the window.

DAY 5

DOWN TO CAVE CITY

Southern Kentucky is home to the planet's longest cave system, with miles of underground world to explore, and many more that humans have yet to see.

On the surface, Cave City has the spirit of a timeworn but tenacious carnival barker. Drive through town, and for every abandoned arcade or dilapidated haunted house, there's also a front yard that's been blanketed in astroturf and turned into a two-hole miniature golf course with a drive-through souvenir stand. But look behind the curtain of roadside kitsch, and MAMMOTH CAVE, the world's largest cave system, which settlers started exploring in the late 1790s, remains a wonder to behold. For amateur spelunkers, the FROZEN NIAGARA TOUR has the biggest payoff for the least tread—hike less than half a mile to reach the massive flowstone deposit that appears like a raging waterfall suspended in stone. FAT MAN'S MISERY presents a more challenging route in the form of a narrow keyhole-shaped passage that a 19th-century visitor described as "an avenue of torture in ruggedness." Once above ground, ditch the protein bar in favor of a sirloin sandwich and a homemade whoopie pie from the Amish-owned FARMWALD'S DUTCH BAKERY before following U.S. 31W to nearby HORSE CAVE and on to the zipline across the sinkhole entrance of HIDDEN RIVER CAVE. To admire the aforementioned from a safe distance, there are always the AMERICAN CAVE MUSEUM's exhibits about bats, blindfish and prehistoric cave explorers.

MORE THAN 30 ENTRIES ⊳
Excerpts have been edited for clarity and concision.

ALMANAC

A deep dive into the cultural heritage of
Kentucky through news clippings, timelines,
writings and other historical hearsay

MUHAMMAD ALI

Louisville *Courier-Journal*
February 25, 1964

CASSIUS LOSES RING CROWN—BEFORE BOUT

MIAMI—Cassius Clay lost the first round of his world heavyweight boxing championship bout yesterday, more than 24 hours before the scheduled starting time, when Morris Klein, Miami Beach boxing commissioner, told him: "If you enter that ring wearing a crown or trying any other monkey business, I'll impound your purse." That was hitting the fun-loving Clay where it hurts most, and he quickly withdrew his announced plans to wear a large shining crown, to be accompanied by two beautiful girls dressed as queens, and to address the crowd on his plans as the next champion while waiting for Sonny Liston to appear. Said Klein, "I've run seven championships here. I haven't allowed any crazy stuff yet and don't intend to start now." Desmond Hackett, a correspondent for the *London Daily Express*, was standing nearby. "I couldn't agree more," he said crisply. "Clay wore a crown when he entered the ring against Henry Cooper in London. It was a very vulgar display, I must say." … Roy Ullyett, a cartoonist, also from the *Daily Express*, nodded agreement. "Such silliness only accentuates the boy-versus-man image this meeting is creating," said Ullyett, pulling his handlebar mustache, the manliest hirsute appendage on the beach. "If I owned Clay's contract, I wouldn't allow that garrulous young parrot to even attend the same tea with a brute like Liston." While virtually everybody, including the Britishers, are picking Liston to win by anything from the breeze of his first swing of the opening round to a 15-round decision, it still remains a possibility that Clay may give the world one of the biggest upsets in boxing history.

> *Born Cassius Clay in Louisville,* MUHAMMAD ALI *did indeed defeat Liston to claim his first world heavyweight title. He soon announced his change of name, a few years after his conversion to Islam, and became one of the world's most famed athletes.*

THE NIGHT RIDERS

In the early 1900s, the monopoly American Tobacco Company slashed prices for the crop. Horseback-mounted farmers called The Night Riders terrorized others within the Black Patch growing district to keep them from selling at the ruinous rate.

NIGHT RIDERS GROW DEFIANT
The Hustler, Madisonville, Kentucky

Hopkinsville, Ky: Feb. 27, 1908—In a stone's throw of the city limits night riders early this morning set fire to the residence of Broussais Gregory. Mr. Gregory's wife and baby were awakened by smoke in the room. With the assistance of a servant the fire was extinguished, but the night riders returned, fired on Gregory, and ordered him back in the house. They pulled weatherboarding from the bedroom, used coal oil plentifully and again set fire to the building. Mrs. Gregory started to the telephone, and being seen by the band, was fired on, but not wounded. The house was riddled with bullets, but Mr. Gregory finally called up relatives in Hopkinsville. ... The night riders had mounted horses and disappeared before the military reached the house. ... The soldiers found a note at the front gate addressed to Gregory, reading: "You sold your tobacco out of the association and we have come to burn you out. If you try to raise anymore tobacco what we will do to you will be a plenty."

> *Guthrie, Kentucky-born Robert Penn Warren wrote about the Black Patch Tobacco Wars in his first novel,* Night Rider, *in 1939. He won the Pulitzer Prize with* All the King's Men, *and twice more for his poem collections. He is the only person to win the prize in fiction and poetry.*

MY OLD KENTUCKY HOME

For a century at the Kentucky Derby, "My Old Kentucky Home" by Stephen Foster has played as the horses come out from the stable. Foster wrote it in the 1850s to speak out against enslavers separating families. In the early 20th century, the song became popular among white audiences at minstrel shows, with some changes to the lyrics, and in 1928, Kentucky adopted it as its state song. Nowadays, the version performed at Churchill Downs replaces a racial slur with "people": *The time has come when the people have to part, / Then my old Kentucky home, good night.*

COUNTRY AND BLUEGRASS MUSICIANS

Central and Eastern Kentucky claim to have produced more hit country and bluegrass artists per capita than any other place in the U.S. Below, lyrics from a few noted artists.

"Well, I was borned a coal miner's daughter / In a cabin, on a hill in Butcher Holler / We were poor but we had love / That's the one thing that daddy made sure of / He shoveled coal to make a poor man's dollar"

LORETTA LYNN "Coal Miner's Daughter."

Lynn grew up near Van Lear. Her sister is the singer Crystal Gale.

"We were waltzing that night in Kentucky / Beneath the beautiful harvest moon / And I was the boy who was lucky / But it all ended too soon / As I sit here alone in the moonlight / I see your smiling face / And I long once more for your embrace / In that beautiful Kentucky waltz"

BILL MONROE "Kentucky Waltz"

Monroe, born in Rosine, was the youngest of his family's eight children.

"And Daddy won't you take me back to Muhlenberg County / Down by the Green River where Paradise lay / Well, I'm sorry, my son, but you're too late in asking / Mister Peabody's coal train has hauled it away"

JOHN PRINE "Paradise"

Prine titled the song after his parents' hometown, where he spent summers.

"I'd give anything to go back / Days I was young / All the way back to Pan Bowl / I sit down on the lakebed / Stare at the sun / Then I'd walk out in the water / Let it cleanse my soul / Spend my days up on Quicksand / There I would play / Wild as a rattlesnake / Right from the start / I'd push August in / Swing all day / Well she was the first girl that ever broke my heart"

STURGILL SIMPSON "Pan Bowl"

Simpson is from Jackson, a small town on the Kentucky River.

> *Singer-songwriter Tom T. Hall on his 1968 hit single "Harper Valley P.T.A.": "It's a true story. I was just a fly on the wall. I was only 8, 9 or 10 years old at the time. ... The lady was a really free spirit, modern way beyond the times in my hometown ... Olive Hill, Ky., pop. 1,300."*

JIM BEAM

Mila Kunis is just the latest in a long list of celebrities who have appeared in the brand's advertisements. A list from a particularly golden period.

SEAN CONNERY 1966-1974 Posed with a bottle and the copy "The taste is distinctive. The man is Sean Connery. The Bourbon is JIM BEAM." Also mentions his most recent flick as James Bond [who preferred martinis, but who cares?].

....

ORSON WELLES 1970-1975 Photographed alongside his daughter Rebecca. Text reads: "Generation gap? Jim Beam never heard of it."

....

ROBERT WAGNER & BETTE DAVIS 1972-1973 The two actors stand side by side smiling with what look more like glasses of iced tea and the same "Generation gap?" question. Compares them and brand to uncompromising love for the craft.

....

BABE RUTH 1974 The Sultan of Swat looks into the bright lights of a stadium above the words "Jim Beam. You can't improve on the original."

....

ELLA FITZGERALD 1974 A turtleneck-sporting First Lady of Song holds up a glass to the message "Two one-of-a-kind originals."

KENTUCKY DERBY WINNERS

A selection of memorable names that have been laureled in roses.

1876 ....Vagrant	1970 ....Dust Commander
1893 ....Lookout	1973 ....Secretariat
1901 ....His Eminence	1982 ....Gato Del Sol
1909 ....Wintergreen	1989 ....Sunday Silence
1914 ....Old Rosebud	1994 ....Go For Gin
1921 ....Behave Yourself	1998 ....Real Quiet
1925 ....Flying Ebony	2004 ....Smarty Jones
1932 ....Burgoo King	2009 ....Mine That Bird
1947 ....Jet Pilot	2012 ....I'll Have Another
1962 ....Decidedly	2019 ....Country House

LOUISVILLE SLUGGER BASEBALL BATS

HUNTER S. THOMPSON

"Just keep in mind for the next few days that we're in Louisville, Kentucky. Not London. Not even New York. This is a weird place." This is what Hunter S. Thompson said to Ralph Steadman, lifelong illustrator of Thompson's bizarro adventures, when they landed at the Kentucky Derby in 1970. Thompson's piece, "The Kentucky Derby is Decadent and Depraved," was published in a short-lived radical magazine called *Scanlan's*. In wild prose, it lampooned the glitzy affair of the Derby and revealed a macabre, absurd layer just beneath the surface. Thompson thought its publication would signal the end of his career. It did very much the opposite. He told *Playboy* in 1974, "It was like falling down an elevator shaft and landing in a pool full of mermaids." It marked Thompson's crossing of the Rubicon from his traditional attempts at journalism to what would come to define his art and his entire persona: "gonzo," a form of fever-dream first-person journalism pulled off with manic flourish. Even before that dispatch, Thompson had trained critical eyes on his home state. In a 1963 article, "A Southern City with Northern Problems," he questioned Louisville's boasts of progress—desegregation in schools and an ordinance outlawing racism in any "public accommodation." Louisville is still slowly coming to terms with this literary icon and self-described "lazy hillbilly." When Thompson died by suicide in 2005, the Louisville *Courier-Journal*, the state's biggest newspaper, gave his death a single column. Now the annual city gathering GonzoFest is in its 10th year.

THE GREAT GATSBY

Step into the lobby of downtown Louisville's Seelbach Hotel and it's not hard to imagine Daisy Buchanan descending the gilded, sapphire-carpeted staircase. According to hotel lore, F. Scott Fitzgerald met the charismatic bootlegger George Remus at this beaux arts beauty when he went out for USO events while stationed at Camp Zachary Taylor, and found his Jay Gatsby. In fact it's quite easy to fall into the dream that Fitzgerald outlined the novel's first draft on a cocktail napkin in the basement bar, The Rathskeller. But it's difficult not to argue with the timing. Fitzgerald was only stationed in Kentucky for a month in 1918. Prohibition was still two years away. It's almost certain he and Remus never clinked glasses. But the Seelbach did make an impression on the author, and even received a name check in chapter four: "By the next autumn [Daisy] was gay again, gay as ever. She had a début after the armistice, and in February she was presumably engaged to a man from New Orleans. In June she married Tom Buchanan of Chicago, with more pomp and circumstance than Louisville ever knew before. He came down with a hundred people in four private cars, and hired a whole floor of the Seelbach Hotel, and the day before the wedding he gave her a string of pearls valued at three hundred and fifty thousand dollars."

MAD MEN

A man walks into a bar. He happens to be Don Draper, ad exec [a.k.a. Dick Whitman, foundling, played with easy-but-weary style by Jon Hamm]. The central figure of *Mad Men* wants an old fashioned. Behind the bar, a man in white evening-dress complains that there's no bourbon. Draper vaults over the bar, swinging his shiny dress shoes, and gets to work making a drink and—or so legend will tell—changing an industry. In the real-life bourbon world, *Mad Men*'s seven seasons [2007-2015] are seen as a turning point, the prestige show that taught America to drink brown liquor again. ["Rye okay with you?" Draper asks his drinking companion.] As business explanations go, it feels a bit folkloric. But the numbers look good: by 2020, bourbon sales had quadrupled over two decades with no end to the upswing in sight. Don Draper *did* make those amber drinks look mighty good, and you *did* want to join him—even if it might be best not to think too hard about what, exactly, old Don was looking for as he stared into the glass.

HEMP FARMING

From early days through World War II, Kentucky led American hemp production. The industry's greatest advocate was the Whig senator [and big-time hemp farmer] Henry Clay.

1811 "With regard to Hemp I feel all the solicitude that belongs to this great staple of our Country. In the Senate, we are precluded constitutionally from introducing a bill which would impose a duty. The other House has had its attention slightly drawn to the subject, and it will be pressed upon them again by our delegation. But such are the jarring interest & views which pervade the National Legislature that I fear nothing effectual will be done."

1837 "I received your obliging letter of the 31 ult. with the paper of hemp seed to which it refers, and for which I request your acceptance of my cordial thanks. It has reached me in good time to have it sowed at the best period [which is from the 20th April to the 10th May], and which I will have carefully done. I hope that the result of the experiment may be the naturalization of a new and valuable variety of hemp in our country."

1842 "I'm going to rig the Navy with cordage made of American Hemp— Kentucky Hemp—Ashland Hemp."

Clay's farm at Ashland, where enslaved people worked to grow the senator's crops, is now maintained as a historic landmark. The farm began growing hemp again in 2016.

MILK

Though Kentucky doesn't even break the top 25 in terms of milk-producing states, milk has been the state beverage since 2005, when Joey Pendleton, state senator and dairy farmer from Hopkinsville, proposed Senate Bill 93, asking legislators to designate milk as the state's official drink. A 2017 petition that deigned to call milk "bland and boring" sought to remove milk as Kentucky's top drink and replace it with bourbon, "a source of pride for its citizens, a major economic driver, and conjures an idyllic image of our state in the minds of those who might choose to visit or do business here."

Country Ham

Ale-8-One

Benedictine

Mint Julep

Sorghum Syrup

Burgoo

Apple Stack Cake

Arroz con Pollo

Sushi

KENTUCKY FOODWAYS OF NOTE

ALE-8-ONE State's official soda. Lemon-lime-tinged ginger ale in kelly-green bottle. George Lee Wainscott originally named it Roxa-Cola after wife Roxanne.

APPLE STACK CAKE Cast-iron-cooked layers baked with molasses or sorghum syrup. Piled up high with spiced-apple puree in between.

ARROZ CON POLLO Also goes by the name ACP. Simple chicken-and-rice combo has been Kentuckified with melty white queso on top.

BEER CHEESE Legend has it the roux-based cheddar dip was surreptitiously served with pretzels to get customers thirsty for more beer.

BENEDICTINE SPREAD Kentucky's answer to broader Southern favorite, pimento cheese. Cream cheese, mayo, cucumber, green onion, dill, lemon juice whipped together. Crudités, crackers—any vehicle works, really.

BURGOO Bluegrass variation on universal hunter's stew. Tomato-backed broth [some add bourbon too] with pork, chicken, veal, lamb, beans, potatoes. Long simmer, no shortcuts.

COUNTRY HAM Before refrigerators, Kentuckians preserved hams with salt and time. Slices often served on biscuits for breakfast. Well-aged ones prized.

GOETTA German pork-and-beef sausage made with steel-cut oats. A good sear on both sides essential.

HOT BROWN Knife-and-fork-required sandwich. Turkey, tomatoes, bacon, Mornay sauce. Open-faced, toasted, and—wait for it—broiled.

MINT JULEP Adulterated versions abound, especially those snow-capped in powdered sugar. The classic, far from overrated: frosted silver cup, muddled mint, fine bourbon, simple syrup, crushed ice.

SORGHUM SYRUP Boiled down from cash-crop grain. Thick and sweet like molasses, with tangy, earthy top note.

SUSHI Kentucky's Japanese transplants, many coming to work at Asian car manufacturers' stateside plants, brought hand rolls and nigiri with them.

TRANSPARENT PIE A chess-style predecessor with opaque filling. Think pecan pie without the nuts.

ABRAHAM LINCOLN

Born on Sinking Spring Farm in Hodgenville, Kentucky, Abraham Lincoln rose from a log cabin to the White House and became one of the world's most consequential leaders. In the lead up to the Civil War, many Southerners called upon Lincoln to "calm the storm" of secession by appeasing politicians and citizens who were in favor of slavery. Below, a speech he wrote in response to a letter, signed "All Kentucky," that expressed such sentiments.

"Again, it is urged as if the word must be spoken before the fourth of March. Why? Is the speaking the word a *sine qua non* to the inauguration? Is there a Bell-man, a Breckinridge-man, or a Douglas man, who would tolerate his own candidate to make such terms, had he been elected? Who amongst you would not die by the proposition, that your candidate, being elected, should be inaugurated, solely on the conditions of the Constitution, and laws, or not at all. What Kentuckian, worthy of his birth-place, would not do this? Gentlemen, I too, am a Kentuckian. Nor is this a matter of mere personal honor. No man can be elected President without some opponents, as well as supporters; and if when elected, he can not be installed, till he first appeases his enemies, by breaking his pledges, and betraying his friends, this government, and all popular government, is already at an end. Demands for such surrender, once recognized, and yielded to, are without limit, as to nature, extent, or repetition. They break the only bond of faith between public, and public servant; and they distinctly set the minority over the majority. Such demands acquiesced in, would not merely be the ruin of a man, or a party; but as a precedent, they would ruin the government itself. I do not deny the possibility that the people may err in an election; but if they do, the true remedy is in the next election, and not in the treachery of the person elected. ... In such case they would all see, that such surrender would not be merely the ruin of a man, or a party; but, as a precedent, would be the ruin of the government itself."

Jefferson Davis, the president of the Confederacy during the Civil War, was born in 1808, in Fairview, Kentucky, just eight months before Lincoln and only 125 miles away from Hodgenville.

FIRST DISTILLERS

DR. JAMES C. CROW 1789-1856

First to use sour mash to accelerate fermentation. Founded Old Crow whiskey, the most popular of its era. Also pioneered first "brand name" by producing barrels with name visible. Ulysses S. Grant, Abraham Lincoln, Mark Twain all professed affection for the brand.

....

GEORGE GARVIN BROWN 1846-1917

Pharmacist and Old Forester founder was the first to sell whiskey in sealed glass bottles rather than dispensed from a barrel. A big-time marketing innovation, as bottled whiskey was touted as higher quality.

....

BASIL HAYDEN 1743-1804

Born into wealthy Catholic family from Maryland, settled in today's Bardstown. Grandson started Old Grand-Dad whiskey to honor him. Jim Beam introduced their Hayden-named bourbon in 1992.

....

COLONEL EDMUND HAYNES TAYLOR JR. 1830-1923 Descendant of two presidents deemed the father of "Modern Bourbon Industry." Taylor lobbied for Bottled-in-Bond Act and built a true distillery around his operation, now operating under name Castle & Key.

COUNTRY HAM

Another example of patience as a key ingredient in Bluegrass foodways, this dry-cured piece of pork has a long Kentucky legacy, all the way back to pioneer days before refrigeration. Traditionally, country ham is made from the hind leg of a pig that's been raised on a diet of acorns, beans, clover and grain. It's packed in a mixture of salts, sugar and spices; cured for anywhere from months to years [depending on the fat content]; and later smoked over a fire of corn cobs, hickory wood or applewood. The hams are not fully cooked but preserved by the cure, much like lox. There are fancy country hams—Broadbent B & B Foods' champion ham went at auction for $2.8 million at the 2018 Kentucky State Fair—to hole-in-the-wall spots that still treasure the time-honored process. And of course, this being Kentucky, there are even hams cured in bourbon rickhouses. Slice it, shave it, put it on a hot, buttery biscuit. Just don't confuse country ham with city ham, wet-cured and often referred to as just "ham."

BREONNA TAYLOR

Asleep next to her boyfriend, Kenneth Walker, Breonna Taylor awoke to Louisville police officers breaking down her door after midnight on March 13, 2020. Thinking the intruder might be Taylor's ex-boyfriend, Walker shot his gun at one of the officers as the door came down, and the officers returned fire. At least eight of those bullets struck Taylor, and police left her gasping, then lifeless on the floor for 20 minutes. An ambulance arrived for the 26-year-old emergency medical technician, but she had already died, likely minutes after the first shots were exchanged. Although that fact, among many, remains unclear, as the officers involved left their incident report almost blank. In the wake of George Floyd's murder in Minneapolis during a summer filled with protests across the country, marchers resurrected Taylor's name. It became a rallying cry within the Black Lives Matter movement—"Arrest the cops that killed Breonna Taylor" echoing across the physical and virtual realms; "Say her name!" pleaded over town squares, in front of government buildings, in city streets. Oprah Winfrey, whose face had been the constant across 241 covers of her *O* magazine, gave the September 2020 issue spotlight to Taylor, saying, "She was just like me. She was just like you." *Vanity Fair* also dedicated its Ta-Nehisi Coates-edited September issue to Taylor, with a cover painted by Amy Sherald, best known for her captivating, unorthodox portraits of President Barack Obama and Michelle Obama. Taylor appears in serene azure and a similarly regal pose as the first lady. In a pages-long interview with Coates [titled "A Beautiful Life"] Taylor's mother Tamika Palmer explains that as protests inflamed Louisville, the mayor asked her to help him quell the rage. "I'm ecstatic that these people are standing up and demanding justice and saying her name. On the other hand, I don't want people to be hurt. I don't want y'all to tear up the city. We still got to live here. And still I understand the anger. ... But I don't do it. Because I know the people don't want to hear from me. They want to hear from him. They aren't looking for me. They want to talk to him. That's his fight, not mine." Despite ongoing press coverage and national conversation, detectives Myles Cosgrove, Joshua Jaynes and Brett Hankinson and Sergeant Jonathan Mattingly have still not faced criminal consequences since their respective terminations. Still, some progress has been made. Almost a year later, Kentucky instituted significant limits statewide on no-knock warrants like the one served at Taylor's home, while the city of Louisville has banned them entirely under "Breonna's Law."

ALICE ALLISON DUNNIGAN

In 1947, the first Black woman reporter with White House credentials, Alice Allison Dunnigan, left her first presidential news conference with Harry S. Truman [after arriving an hour early] and thought to herself, "You've come a long way, sister." In her autobiography, *A Black Woman's Experience: From Schoolhouse to White House*, Dunnigan acknowledged she was far from "the ramshackle, unpainted, one room schoolhouse tucked away at the edge of a scrubby, unsightly thicket on a red clay hill in rural Logan County." It was there she had written her first book, *The Fascinating Story of Black Kentuckians*, compiled when she found her students completely unaware of the contributions of African Americans in the state. After taking a job as a typist in D.C., Dunnigan's tenacity earned her a role as a correspondent for the Associated Negro Press. Although she secured a press pass to cover almost every hall of government and traveled with President Truman's press corps, she would at the same time regularly pawn her watch to make rent. Dunnigan eventually left the press for a role in Lyndon B. Johnson's administration. In a letter to her editor, Claude Barnett, dated 1948, she wrote, "If I can so live to inspire others to strive to achieve, I will not have lived my life in vain." Aspiration achieved.

FORT KNOX

"50 ARMED TRAINS TO TAKE GOLD TO KENTUCKY VAULT"
The Paducah Sun-Democrat, August 8, 1936

Well-informed sources said today that 50 or more armored trains may be required to move the bulk of Uncle Sam's $10,600,000,000 gold hoard into the strong box now nearing completion at Fort Knox, Ky. ... The transfer of the precious metal to the Fort Knox vault, which Treasury officials say will be impregnable to safe-blowers and even a well-equipped army, is part of a long term program to shift gold reserves from seaboard cities to points far in the interior. Last year more than $2,000,000,000 in bullion was moved from San Francisco to a vault at the Denver mint, where the government considered it would be safe from any threat, including invasion by a foreign foe. ... The Treasury house itself combines the most modern construction with a few characteristics of the medieval castle. ... At the touch of a button, [its] water can be released to fill underground vaults where the yellow bars will be hidden.

BARN QUILTS

A stretch of Southern Kentucky road called the Warren County Quilt Trail exhibits many folk art representations of a treasured Kentucky craft—quilts—painted on barns.

SUNFLOWER .... Joseph & Karen Porter
3074 Browning Rd, Rockfield

LONE STAR .... Dale & Peggy Tucker
3877 Matlock Rd, Bowling Green

GOOSE TRACKS & ROAD TO FORTUNE .... Dale & Peggy Tucker
5037 Richpond Rd, Bowling Green

KENTUCKY STAR .... Ted & Nadine Pemberton
250 Ted Pemberton Rd, Bowling Green

SEVEN STARS OR SEVEN SISTERS .... Wade & Chryl Johnson
7179 Plano Rd, Bowling Green

GRAMMIE QUILT .... Bill & Peggy Klein
565 Lillard Rd, Bowling Green [dead-end road]

OLD RELIABLES .... Robert and Freida Moore
1251 Goodrum Rd, Bowling Green

WAVE QUILT .... Gary Willoughby
12383 Woodburn Allen Springs Rd, Alvaton

STARLIGHT .... Nancy Hill
12834 Alvaton Scottsville Rd, Alvaton

AMERICANA LONE STAR .... Tom & Nancy Lobenstein
8346 Nob Hill Rd, Alvaton

LONE STAR .... Jo Jean Scott
565 Colette Bridge Rd, Bowling Green

BEAR'S CLAW .... David & Janice Robertson
3633 Old Greenhill Rd, Bowling Green

LEAF PATTERN .... Norris & Mary Thomas
2162 Old Greenhill Rd, Bowling Green [black barn right on road]

AMERICA'S SALVATION .... Gerald & Ann Smith
530 Hunts Lane, Bowling Green

TOBACCO LEAF .... Robert & Sue Donoho
495 Hays Rd, Bowling Green

ADOLPH RUPP

"Bravo for the Baron"
Sports Illustrated, March 7, 1966

A governor cannot succeed himself in the Commonwealth of Kentucky, and a horse can run only once in the Derby, but as long as Adolph Rupp is around the Bluegrass will never suffer from a lack of continuity. For 36 years, in a land of colonels, he has been the only Baron, a man of consummate pride and well-earned privilege. One might think that Adolph Rupp would be satisfied now to retire to his estate in the pleasant, rolling country outside Lexington, there to tend his prize Herefords and Burley tobacco, to rest amid his affluence and such souvenirs of glory as no other basketball coach ever has gathered. Instead, at the age of 64, he continues to pursue the only challenge left—trying to top himself. And that is some tough act to follow. Rupp has won 743 games, 22 Southeastern Conference titles [the trophy shown with him on the cover represents one of these] and four NCAA national championships, as well as enough acclaim [and censure, too] to serve most men, barons and otherwise, for all their years. Yet his persistence in staying at his job has won him this year something more than just another trophy or a few fresh statistics. He is threatening to become the grand old man of basketball.

Adolph Rupp coached the University of Kentucky men's basketball team from 1930 to 1972, embedding fast-break offense and championship victories deep in Commonwealth culture. Just weeks after this profile by Frank Deford, Rupp's all-white Wildcats lost the NCAA championship to an all-Black squad from Texas Western. UK's team integrated in 1971.

WATERFALLS

A selection of names from the state's near 900 waterfalls.

THREE SISTERS	YAHOO	PRINCESS
DOG SLAUGHTER	SEVENTY SIX	MYSTERY
STAR CREEK	REDEMPTION	JOCK

BOURBON BRANDS

Below, a brief key to which companies currently own which distilleries and the umbrella brands they produce. *Denotes distillery

BEAM SUNTORY
Jim Beam*
Basil Hayden's
Booker's
Knob Creek
Old Crow
Old Grand-Dad
Maker's Mark*

BROWN-FORMAN
Early Times
Old Forester
Woodford Reserve*

DIAGEO
Bulleit*

HEAVEN HILL DISTILLERIES, INC.
Cabin Still
Elijah Craig
Evan Williams
Fighting Cock
Heaven Hill
J.T.S. Brown
Old Fitzgerald
Old Heaven Hill

KENTUCKY BOURBON DISTILLERS, LTD.
Johnny Drum
Old Bardstown
Kentucky Vintage
Noah's Mill
Rowan's Creek
Vintage Bourbon

Willett Pot Still Reserve
Old Pogue

KIRIN
Four Roses*

LUXCO
Ezra Brooks
Old Ezra 101
Rebel Yell
Yellowstone

SAZERAC
Barton 1792*
1792 Ridgemont Reserve
Kentucky Gentleman
Kentucky Tavern
Ten High
Very Old Barton
Ancient Age
Blanton's
Buffalo Trace*
Eagle Rare
George T. Stagg
Old Charter
E.H. Taylor
Van Winkle
Rock Hill Farms
W.L. Weller

WILD TURKEY
Wild Turkey*
Russell's Reserve
Longbranch

THOMAS MERTON

*An American Trappist monk, writer, theologian, mystic and poet, as well as a
staunch social activist, Thomas Merton was a member of the Abbey of Our Lady
of Gethsemani, near Bardstown, Kentucky, and lived there from 1941 until his
death in 1968. A marker commemorating one of his spiritual epiphanies on
Walnut Street is located in downtown Louisville.*

"In Louisville, at the corner of Fourth and Walnut, in the center of the
shopping district, I was suddenly overwhelmed with the realization that I
loved all those people, that they were mine and I theirs, that we could not
be alien to one another even though we were total strangers. It was like
waking from a dream of separateness, of spurious self-isolation in a special world, the world of renunciation and supposed holiness. ... This sense
of liberation from an illusory difference was such a relief and such a joy
to me that I almost laughed out loud. ... I have the immense joy of being
man, a member of a race in which God Himself became incarnate. As if
the sorrows and stupidities of the human condition could overwhelm me,
now that I realize what we all are. And if only everybody could realize this!
But it cannot be explained. There is no way of telling people that they are
all walking around shining like the sun. ... Then it was as if I suddenly saw
the secret beauty of their hearts, the depths of their hearts, where neither
sin nor desire nor self-knowledge can reach, the core of their reality, the
person that each one is in God's eyes. If only they could all see themselves
as they really are. If only we could see each other that way all the time."

DANIEL BOONE

From Lord Byron's *Don Juan* to Fess Parker's 1960s TV portrayal, American frontiersman Daniel Boone occupies national consciousness as a
hulking, buckskin-clad figure, raccoon-skin cap atop his head. But Boone
was far from the man who fought off wolves with his bare hands. "Nothing embitters my old age," he said, "more than the circulation of absurd
stories. ... With me the world has taken great liberties, and yet I have been
but a common man." Raised a Quaker, Boone was more prone to pacifism
than battle, and as a surveyor, his maps left followers wanting. Still, he
really did explore Kentucky in the late 1700s when the future commonwealth lay beyond the 13 colonies. Today, many rugged places in the U.S.
carry his name, including Daniel Boone National Forest.

TOM BULLOCK

The son of a formerly enslaved man turned Union soldier, Louisville-born Tom Bullock was a pre-Prohibition bartender and author of 1917 cocktail recipe book *The Ideal Bartender*. Bullock occupied a unique liminal space for a Black person at the time, interacting with customers such as Theodore Roosevelt and presidential ancestor George Herbert Walker [who wrote the forward for his book]. Below, the recipe for his Kentucky-style mint julep, likely created while he was working at Louisville's Pendennis Club.

MINT JULEP: KENTUCKY STYLE

Use a large Silver Mug

Dissolve one lump of Sugar in one-half pony of Water.
Fill mug with Fine Ice.

Two jiggers of Old Bourbon Whiskey.

Stir well; add one bouquet of Mint and serve.

Be careful and not bruise the Mint.

EMPTY LANDSCAPE MYTH

Indigenous peoples have lived in and moved through the land now known as Kentucky for at least 10,000 years. Area tribes at the time of statehood included the Cherokee, Chickasaw, Chippewa, Delaware, Eel River, Haudenosaunee, Kaskaskia, Kickapoo, Miami, Ottawa, Piankeshaw, Potawatomi, Shawnee, Wea and Wyandot. So why did the belief that Kentucky was "empty" when settlers arrived gain so much traction? The myth can be traced in part to John Filson, a land speculator who claimed in his book *The Discovery, Settlement and Present State of Kentucke* [published in 1784, four years before Filson's death] that there were no Native Americans living in Kentucky. Filson and others like him pushed the idea that the land was unoccupied to encourage farmers to settle there. In the decades that followed, other historians and settlers repeated Filson's claim. The 1830 Indian Removal Act—and the "Trail of Tears" that followed—further erased Indigenous identities, as those who stayed behind were forced to hide and therefore omitted from official records. Moreover, the splitting of Kentucky society into "white" and "colored" in the 19th century left Native Americans out of the narrative, in what historians have called "documentary genocide."

COAL

1750 ..... Explorer, physician Thomas Walker discovers coal in land that will become Kentucky and uses it to heat campfire

1790 ..... Earliest known commercial coal production of 20 tons in Lee County, two years before Kentucky statehood

1813 ..... Kentucky produces over 1,000 tons of coal

1848 .... First coal miners' union forms in Schuykill County, PA

1855 ..... Kentucky's annual coal production exceeds 100,000 tons

1860s... Civil War briefly diverts coal production from Kentucky to coalfields of Pennsylvania, Maryland, Ohio and Illinois

1870s... A growing economy increases demand for Kentucky coal; railroads are built in Eastern and Western Kentucky coalfields to boost delivery efficiency

1879 ..... Kentucky's coal production exceeds one million tons for first time

1890 .... United Mine Workers of America formed

1916 ..... Child labor laws prohibit the interstate sale of goods produced by miners under the age of 16

1917 ..... War declared on Germany. President Wilson creates United States Fuel Administration to encourage increased coal production.

1969 ..... Federal Coal Mine Health and Safety Act put into law

1970 ..... Federal Clean Air Act passed

1980 .... Study of acid rain underway with enactment of National Acid Precipitation Assessment Program. Western coalfields found to produce lower-heating coal also higher in sulfur content.

1988 ..... Wyoming overtakes Kentucky as the leading coal producer

1990 .... United States Clean Air Act amendments pass, establishing limits for sulfur dioxide and nitrous oxide from coal-fired power plants

1990 .... Kentucky coal production peaks at over 173 million tons

1997 ..... Kentucky Fish and Wildlife Commission votes to reintroduce elk into 14 Eastern Kentucky counties on post-mined lands, citing mountaintop removal areas and old mine benches as good habitat

1998 ..... 10,000 miners out of work due to mechanized coal removal

2011 ..... Democratic Governor Steve Beshear tells E.P.A to "get off our backs" in regard to mountaintop removal mining. Wendell Berry part of massive sit-in at Beshear's office protesting destructive practice.

2019 .... Harlan County coal miners organize labor protest against Blackjewel over unpaid wages following company's bankruptcy, occupying railroad line for two months. Senator Bernie Sanders sends pizza to protesters.

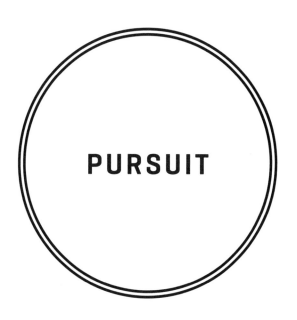

PURSUIT

A field guide to bourbon in Kentucky, from distilleries to bars, with historical background, cultural insight, tasting advice and stories from the figures who make and pour it

BOURBON HISTORY

In Kentucky, layers of geological development provided a sturdy foundation for the first distillers to bring the spirit from barn potstills to the world. Today, bourbon making stands as one of the country's most storied traditions, filled with family legacies, technical expertise and commitment to craft.

FOUNDATIONS

CULTURE

Contrary to liquor lore, early distillers didn't come to Kentucky to avoid George Washington's tax during the Whiskey Rebellion. Rather, distilling was a natural extension of the agrarian society immigrants [Jewish Europeans, Welsh, Scottish, Irish, German, English and French] established as early settlers. Once the art of distilling was refined and regulated, spirit-making was professionalized, and the modern Kentucky bourbon industry was born. Today there are more than 35 working bourbon distilleries in Kentucky, down from the hundreds, perhaps thousands, of stills from frontier days, but up from just eight that were operational 20 years ago.

CLIMATE

Kentucky's long growing season makes it ripe territory for cultivating grains and corn necessary for a bourbon mash bill. Underground, the area's water tables are filtered through limestone, full of nutrients that feed yeast during the fermentation process through hot, humid summers and cold winters. Each season provides the perfect balance for maturing whiskey, pushing it into the charred oak of the barrel in the summertime and pulling it out in the winter. Distinct weather patterns and events can put unique stamps on individual batches as they age in rickhouses.

GEOLOGY

Born of the last ice age, Kentucky's limestone shelf and Ohio River were a boon for bourbon. As glaciers pushed down from the north, limestone on the northern border ground into pebbles and changed the terrain above and underground. The intact shelf created a karst landscape, in which mineral-rich aquifers developed. The river served as an interstate highway system in frontier days, making bourbon marketable elsewhere.

TIMELINE

Approximately 70,000 years ago, glaciers push into Kentucky and eventually melt as global temperatures return to pre-Ice Age levels. This glacial retreat forms the state's rivers and unique water table.

1770s .... European settlers arrive, bringing stills

1818 ...... Catherine Carpenter records recipe for sour mash

1821 ...... First written record of bourbon appears in a KY newspaper

1867 ...... U.S. Secretary of the Treasury adopts use of hydrometer as means to ensure distillers pay tax only on whiskey they sell after aging [not before evaporation] to pay for the Civil War

1870 ..... George Garvin Brown releases Old Forrester [one r today]

1897 ...... Bottled-in-Bond Act passes, which required quality standards

1909 ..... Taft "Decision on Whiskey" says only water can be added to be considered "straight" whiskey

1918 ...... Congress passes first wartime prohibition

1920 ...... Federal Prohibition takes effect. Only six Kentucky distilleries apply for and receive licenses to produce medicinal spirits

1933 .... Prohibition is repealed on December 5

1935 .... Heaven Hill and Stitzel-Weller open; Jim Beam Distillery releases first post-Prohibition batch

1941 ...... Wartime prohibition enacted to support WWII efforts, with brief holiday in 1943 to replenish whiskey stocks

1959 ...... Maker's Mark launches, creates "premium" bourbon category at behest of cofounder Margie Samuels

1964 ..... Congress declares bourbon distinct product of the U.S.A.

1984 ..... Blanton's, first ever single-barrel bourbon, released

1988 ...... Booker Noe coins term "small-batch bourbon"

1994 ..... Jim Rutledge becomes master distiller of Four Roses. Brings brand back to the U.S. after nearly 40 years as export-only.

1999 ...... Kentucky Bourbon Trail founded

2007 ..... *Mad Men* premieres, popularizing bourbon drinking again

2009 ..... Bourbon sales jump 40 percent over the next five years

2016 ...... Wild Turkey hires Matthew McConaughey as a creative director

2021 ...... Around 95 percent of world's bourbon supply still made in Kentucky

MASH BILL & WATER

All bourbon is whiskey, but not any whiskey is bourbon. To earn the name, bourbon must be made from a mash of at least 51 percent corn, distilled no higher than 160 proof, and barreled no higher than 125 proof. It can contain nothing but pure water, yeast, and grains, and must be made on U. S. soil.

Commercial whiskey likely became known as "bourbon" in New Orleans, where whiskey aged in charred barrels, a step common in French spirits, was sold on Bourbon Street. As demand grew, mash bills became signature recipes to definine style and replicate flavor. Below, the most common grains.

CORN	Abundant and affordable. Bills usually list more than 51 percent, 75 being more typical. Most use yellow dent #2, but some distillers use heirloom varieties.
BARLEY	Contains greatest enzymatic potential to convert sugar to alcohol, especially malted barley, which has been soaked and germinated.
RYE	A high-rye bill would list it at around 30 percent. Rye imbues a warming, peppery taste with notes of baking spices.
WHEAT	When rye is swapped for wheat, the character becomes mellower and sweeter. Far less burn.

WATER

Kentucky's karst topography means that groundwater filters through soluble rock formations, namely limestone, which removed impurities and iron and adds minerals that aid fermentation. A higher iron presence in the water would turn bourbon black as it oxidizes. The added calcium and other minerals give Kentucky's water what's said to be a sweet taste. Louisville has one of the oldest and most sophisticated water treatment plants in the U.S. Other municipalities often send their hydrologists and water engineers to the highly decorated facility for research.

PRODUCTION CYCLE

Bourbon's creation combines terroir, time and technical expertise.

HARVEST Most corn used for bourbon, whether it's conventionally grown or an open-pollinated heirloom variety, is harvested mid-August to mid-October. Rye and wheat grow at different times of the year, but barley is a winter crop with a narrow harvest window, as moisture causes sprouting in the field.

....

FERMENTATION Grains are milled and brought to temperature—around 77 degrees—to make the sugars available for fermentation so yeast can thrive. This stage can take anywhere from three to 10 days.

....

DISTILLATION No matter what type of still they use, or if they strain the solids from the previous step, the distiller's point of view comes through at this time. The fully fermented distiller's beer is heated and vapors rise, cool and condense. The higher the distillation proof, the less flavor will come through in the final product.

....

BARRELING Bourbon must be barreled at no more than 125 proof. The 110 to 120 range is most common. Whiskeys on the lower-proof end will take on more wood characteristics earlier on.

....

AGING Proof goes up as bourbon ages in rickhouses under the summer sun, which causes water to evaporate from the barrel. But high humidity can decrease evaporation, especially in stone or brick houses that hold in humidity. A top floor can be 20 degrees hotter than the bottom, so maturation varies depending on placement.

....

BATCHING Master blenders choose barrels to batch together to maintain a consistent identity. Inventory management is just as important to a brand's flavor profile as a mash bill or distillation process.

....

BOTTLING Straight bourbon ages a minimum of two years. Bottled-in-bond must be distilled by the same distiller within the same season, and aged for a minimum of four years. There is no minimum age for bourbon, but if it is under two years old the label must show the exact age.

TASTING

GLASSWARE It might seem over-the-top, but vessel shape has a big impact on flavor perception. The standard whiskey-tasting glass is the Glencairn, with a wide bowl at the bottom and a taper to the top to harness aroma. There are many glasses to choose from—neat and rocks glasses, copita, Norlan, NOS'R—but in a pinch a white-wine glass makes a fine sub. Conducting a serious tasting? Don't mix glasses.

APPEARANCE With a decent pour in a glass, hold it up to the light. Colors range from straw to amber, honey to gold, copper to maple. Sometimes finished whiskeys can even take on reddish hues from the wine casks they rested in. A deeper amber tone typically indicates an older whiskey, but color is not always a great indicator of anything other than the amount of soluble barrel components in the whiskey, as any color imparted comes from the barrel.

AROMA When nosing bourbon, it's important to keep your mouth open so as not to overwhelm the olfactory bulbs in the nasal cavities. Breathe through your mouth to get a more subtle sense of the aromas. Is the vanilla more caramel in character or more like vanilla extract? Are the baking spices more allspice or cinnamon? Is there a fruity or floral note? Smell and taste go in hand in hand with experience and memory, so don't expect to get the same notes as someone else.

THE KENTUCKY CHEW A statewide practice of swishing bourbon all around the inside of your mouth so it coats every taste receptor. Be as animated as is comfortable. Just make sure to coat your palate.

PALATE There's a reason almost every brand has its own tasting wheel to help place words on the sensory spectrum. But the perceived flavors haven't been added. They occur naturally as a result of the entire production process. Yeast can create floral and fruity flavors, grains add spice and nuttiness, and the barrel generally gives woody and candied notes. Viscosity or mouthfeel can heighten or diminish characteristics too.

FINISH Most bourbons split the difference between a long and short finish, with a lingering but not overpowering sensation. Take note of whether the finish is bracing or refreshing. That warm tingle as a sip of bourbon goes down? That's what they call the Kentucky Hug.

BOURBON COLLECTING

A short selection of limited bottles [beyond Pappy] to snatch if spotted, a mix of shelf-space worthy classics and craft kinds to try.

1792 BOTTLED IN BOND

Proof that bourbon needn't be expensive and hard-to-find to be great. This reliable, affordable cult favorite has caramel apple and mint notes.

BOOKER'S BOURBON

Jim Beam's Booker Noe popularized small-batch whiskeys. To honor his legacy, new batches commemorate different people and stories around the brand.

WILD TURKEY MASTER'S KEEP

Master distiller Jimmy Russell started back in 1954, and these releases only get more exquisite with each year of his tenure.

ELIJAH CRAIG BARREL PROOF

Heaven Hill releases one in spring and another in fall. As close to sampling straight from the distillery's rickhouse as it gets.

FOUR ROSES LIMITED EDITION

Markedly different from their standard Small Batch. Hand-numbered bottles contain bourbon picked from 10 different recipes, allowing bolder characters to emerge.

OLD FORESTER 117 SERIES

First Brown-Forman bourbon to bear a woman's signature on the label in the company's 25-year history: that of Master Blender Jackie Zykan.

CLASSIC	CRAFT
W. L. Weller Full Proof	Yellowstone Select Bourbon
Evan Williams Single Barrel	Hartfield & Co. Bourbon
Basil Hayden's Bourbon	Noah's Mill
Henry McKenna Single Barrel	Kentucky Peerless Bourbon
Maker's Mark 46	Jeptha Creed 4-Grain

BESTS

DISTILLERIES

ARCHITECTURE
Four Roses Distillery
Lawrenceburg
Built by famed distillery designers Joseph & Joseph. Spanish Mission-style building [circa 1910] underwent painstaking restoration.

....

STORIED SITE
Stitzel-Weller
Shively
Opened Derby Day 1935. Founded by Pappy Van Winkle himself, later owned by Alex Farnsley and Arthur Stitzel, all of whom put Kentucky bourbon on the map.

....

FARM FOCUS
Jeptha Creed
Shelbyville
Started by mother-daughter distillers Joyce and Autumn Nethery. Centuries-old family farm grows Bloody Butcher corn used in their bourbon.

REVIVED LEGACY
Kentucky Peerless
Louisville
The state's second-largest distillery in its heyday. Taylor family was able to keep their original DSP number, 50, assigned in 1889.

....

NAME RECOGNITION
Jim Beam Clermont Distillery
Clermont
One of the most popular bourbon brands. American Stillhouse tour traces family lineage to seventh-generation distiller Fred Noe.

....

URBAN DISTILLERY
Rabbit Hole Distillery
Louisville
Looks more akin to a contemporary art museum. Founder Kaveh Zamanian stakes his operation on creative, nuanced mash bills.

TOUR TYPES
Buffalo Trace Distillery
Frankfort
Venture into the rickhouses, stroll the gardens, hear ghost stories or put on a hard hat to see the stills and cookers. Acrophobics discouraged.

....

BIG TIME
Heaven Hill Distillery
Bardstown
Bourbon Country's largest distillery, with three tasting rooms. Dramatic tale of how it came to occupy former Bernheim plant.

....

RESTAURANT
Bardstown Bourbon Co.
Bardstown
Gleaming glass facility uniquely built for contract distilling. Menu revolves around farm-sourced Kentucky classics.

WORKING COOPERAGE

Old Forester
Distillery
Louisville

Typically, cooperages and distilleries are separate, but this small-scale operation shows the full process, including raising and charring barrels.

....

CRAFT CULT FOLLOWING

Willett Distillery
Bardstown

Bourbon heads know this name for its Kentucky-only releases Johnny Drum and Old Bardstown, especially the Estate series. Also produces Rowan's Creek.

SMALL-TOWN SPIRIT

Hartfield & Co.
Paris

The first bourbon distillery in Bourbon County after Prohibition. Serious about process, more brewpub in attitude about its place in community.

....

FAMILY DYNASTY

Wild Turkey
Lawrenceburg

Master distiller for 60 years, Jimmy Russell [now in his 80s] is the longest-tenured person under that title. Today, his son Eddie co-runs the show with him.

DISTILLERY BAR

Michter's Fort
Nelson Distillery
Louisville

Devised by noted cocktail historian David Wondrich. Take a drink out to the mezzanine overlooking the microdistillery below.

....

REIMAGINED SPACE

Angel's Envy
Distillery
Louisville

Moved to Louisville's Main Street, known as Whiskey Row, in 2016. Renovated former tool factory and goat racing spot.

BARS

BEGINNERS BAR

Trouble Bar
Louisville

A neighborhood bar first and foremost, with an accessibility-minded ethos [name comes from John Lewis]. Known for expert bartenders who are teachers not preachers. Ace cocktail game.

BOURBON SELECTION

Doc Crow's
Louisville

Boasts a 10-page list with 2,000 varieties.

....

DOUBLE DUTY

Prohibition Bar
Newport

Coffee roaster by day, tasting room by night. Golden shelves of the best bottles.

COZY TASTING ROOM

Amsden Bourbon Bar
Versailles

Historic building. Tufted leather couch for comfy sipping.

....

BUCOLIC BAR

Barn8
Goshen

Inside a barn with design-minded rennovation.

PERSPECTIVES

"To me, the title of Bourbon Steward means when someone sits at my bar, no matter their knowledge, it's my responsibility to help them find a new joy. At Trouble Bar we're not pretentious. There are many people in the city who think that because you don't know much about bourbon or you like your bourbon with Coke or you're a Black female that you must have no earthly idea what you're doing. I love when people come in and just want to have a good experience or try something new without being talked down to. I can do that."

—FELICIA CORBETT, beverage director, Trouble Bar

"Vendome Copper and Brass Works has been in business in Louisville since 1903. Family-run, fourth generation, and I had the privilege of, starting last year, working with the fifth generation. Vendome makes distilling equipment, specifically copper pot stills. I've had my hand in making over 200, easily. Even now, going to the distilleries and seeing the pieces that I worked on and seeing them do their job—that's what made my job worth it."

—SHAWN STEVENS, retired metal worker and unofficial company historian, Vendome Copper & Brass

"I always felt, being a Kentucky woman, that there was a large female market that was just as loyal. We just weren't in conversation with them. So I said, 'Well, I'll start my own thing.' Bourbon Women was born in 2011. We had about 75 women show up and it was one of the most exciting days in my life. Now we have thousands of women."

—PEGGY NOE STEVENS, first female master bourbon taster

"When I was in college, I thought I would do something else with science, like fuel additives or biodiesel or renewable energy. I got this lucky internship working for Brown-Forman and absolutely fell in love with the nerdy, technical side of distilling. I had to be rewired to think more creatively. I joke that if I had just tried to go straight into this industry, I would have built a highly efficient distillery, but the bourbon wouldn't have tasted good. Relearning creativity meant recognizing the trade-offs: sometimes you don't get the best yield, but you get amazing flavor."

—MARIANNE EAVES, Kentucky's first female master distiller

Louisville

frazier

thoroughbred

corn & rye

Hopkinsville

Bardstown

4002

65

64

DISTILLERIES

1. Stitzel-Weller
2. Kentucky Peerless
3. Michter's
4. Old Forester
5. Rabbit Hole
6. Kentucky Artisan

7. Jeptha Creed
8. Bulleit
9. Castle & Key
10. Buffalo Trace
11. Hartfield & Co.
12. James E. Pepper

13. Town Branch
14. Woodford Reserve
15. Wild Turkey
16. Four Roses
17. Maker's Mark
18. Heaven Hill

19. C
20.
21. E
22. J
23. C

horse farm

10

9 ★ Frankfort

capitol

Paris

11

63

9

14

h

13 12

Lexington

Lawrenceburg

Versailles

15

16

Shaker chair

N

W E

S

Lincoln's birthplace

~ BARS, STORES, ETC. ~

a. Frazier Museum

b. Doc Crows

c. Prohibition Craft Spirits Bar & Tours

d. meta

e. Trouble Bar

f. Barr8

g. The Silver Dollar

h. Oma

i. The Old Talbott Tavern

j. Toddy's Liquors

k. Oscar Getz Museum of Whiskey History

INTERVIEWS

---

*Ten conversations with locals of note about poetry,
community theater, family legacies, "Mexington,"
songwriting, matriarchs, racetracks and bourbon*

SAM FORE

CHEF

MY FOLKS CAME over from Sri Lanka in the '70s.

THEY STARTED OUT in New York and ended up in Lexington because my dad got a job with the Veterans Administration. He is 81 and still a VA physician.

THERE WAS A SMALL Sri Lankan community here. That's the interesting thing about Lexington. You're in a city where people speak 36 different languages, but it doesn't always feel like it.

I CAME BACK after nine years in Boston, and I never looked back. Kentucky is a wonderland for me. I love the "What can I do for you?" versus "What can you do for me?"

WHEN MY MOM came here, she didn't know how to cook. Now she's one of the most phenomenal cooks I've known in my life.

BUT SHE HAD to learn. It's not like you come to Kentucky in the '70s expecting wonderful fish and produce right out the gate.

WE WOULD HAVE collard greens stir fried with coconut, and it would be perfect. That developed into some of my favorite dishes.

FOR TUK TUK'S first pop-up, I spent $572. I had no expectations. The first night, we sold out and made $750.

I FOCUSED ON accessibility so that people recognized components and weren't afraid to try anything.

LIKE THE OKRA and tomatoes my family's made for ages. It's very similar to a Southern version; it's just got turmeric, cumin and cardamom.

IT'S AN EXCITING challenge to take over a restaurant or a bar. Showing people dimension and depth beyond salt, pepper and paprika. They get this moment of, "Oh, I know this flavor but I've never had it like this before."

INEVITABLY, somebody's going to try a coconut curry deviled egg just for the hell of it.

FREDDIE JOHNSON

DISTILLERY GUIDE

I STARTED PLAYING at Buffalo Trace Distillery when I was five.

MY GRANDFATHER and Colonel Blanton met on the riverbank behind the distillery as kids.

ONE OF THOSE Tom Sawyer, Huckleberry Finn kind of stories.

THEY WERE HERE together for 52 years, and my grandfather became the first African American to manage the warehouses at a major distillery. At this point, he was managing 250,000 barrels of whiskey.

MY GRANDFATHER brought my dad into the whiskey-making business.

MY DAD AND granddad assumed when I got out of school I would just come to work at Buffalo Trace like they did.

BUT THE BOURBON industry slowed down. For a period of time, we only made 2,000 barrels for the whole year. The warehouses were full of whiskey. Bourbon wasn't moving.

I ENDED UP being a network systems design engineer with AT&T.

I WORKED WITH Bell Labs on designing network reservation systems. I had underground military clearance.

IN THE MIDST of all that, I got a phone call from my dad. He was terminally ill.

HE ASKED ME, would I keep my promise and come back to Frankfort to be his caregiver.

ONCE HE GETS me back to Frankfort, then he says, "Oh, by the way, remember you made me that promise you're going to work at the distillery during my lifetime?"

HE WANTED TO be able to tell people that he had three direct generations who worked in Buffalo Trace Distillery.

WHEN PEOPLE COME in just for a visit to the distillery—they may not be thinking about a tour at the time. They just want to pop in and see what's going on. So, when you encounter these folks you don't really know their baggage.

BUT WHAT I do know is that encounter provides you the opportunity to create what I call "memory moments." And to me, that's what being a guide is all about.

THE FIRST THING I try to get visitors to understand when they come to a place like this is integrity. Integrity is critical, no matter what you do. It doesn't matter your business. It doesn't matter the product you produce. I say, your integrity determines everything.

SOMETIMES MY DAD would come down here to the distillery, and he would have fun with the tourists coming in. He had this old beat-up old car, and he'd pull up next to me on a tour and would say, "Hello everybody." And they'd say, "Hello."

HE'D SAY, "That's my boy giving those tours, and he's still not giving them right." Then he'd laugh and drive off in his car.

WHEN WE WERE drinking that last bottle of the Pappy with him, all these things started to come out.

WHEN WE TALKED, I'm going to tell you, it's crazy. It was the first time that my father and I, and my brother, had spent three hours together, just us.

WE TALKED ABOUT everything. It was just a magical moment.

THAT'S WHEN HE shared with me, he said, "Of all the things you've ever done for me, keeping your promise was the best present you've ever given me."

I HADN'T EVER thought about it that way. I just thought about taking care of my dad.

SILAS HOUSE

AUTHOR

I GREW UP close to Cumberland Falls in a really little town—about 500 people—and I feel like I was kin to most of them.

IT WAS A very matriarchal place, especially when it came to storytelling.

I GREW UP around so many strong women, women who were up against great obstacles. My paternal grandmother raised nine children, from the ages of 1 to 16, by herself working at the first Kentucky Fried Chicken in Corbin.

THINGS LIKE THAT make me feel like I have a real stake in Kentucky history.

MY FIRST BOOK, *Clay's Quilt,* came out 20 years ago this year. It's a very Kentucky story.

THAT'S ONE THING I really wanted to get across was what a complicated place it is, and how often it's seen as a really simple place.

WHEN YOU'RE FROM a state you have to defend all the time, it makes you love it more. You look harder at things you do love about it, and you're able to articulate that pretty easily.

I THINK MOST LGBTQ people from Kentucky and the South would tell you their orientation—and judgment they received for it—is always tangled up with religion.

WHAT I WAS trying to do in my other book, *Southernmost,* was look at the complexities of that.

LOTS OF PEOPLE don't think of gay people as people of faith. I've always been a person of deep faith who also happens to be gay.

I BELIEVE THE role of a novel is to get into those individual complexities and go beyond the generalizations.

EVEN IF YOU have a place where the vast majority is conservative, still within it, you have individuals who have their own thoughts and hearts about what they believe.

MARIAH GARCIA

RACETRACK EMPLOYEE ADVOCATE

I STUDIED FRENCH and Spanish at the University of Louisville. I love languages.

AS PART OF studying Spanish there, I completed an internship with the Kentucky Racing Health Services Center, which is a clinic that serves the racetrack community.

MY ROLE WAS as a volunteer interpreter. Although my Spanish is not perfect—I'm not a native speaker—I improved it there.

SOME PEOPLE ASKED, "Have you ever gone over to La Escuelita?" which means "the little school." That's the pet name for the Backside Learning Center.

I WAS LIKE, "No, I don't know it," and they said, "Oh, you should check it out, I think you would like it."

OFTEN WHEN I say the name, eyebrows get raised, so I have to clarify that the "backside" refers to the backside of the racetrack, where the horses are stabled.

THERE ARE 47 barns and it's a whole world unto itself. A sparkling, beautiful community.

THERE'S ABOUT A thousand people employed at the backside. The grooms, hot walkers, jockeys, exercise riders, all the behind-the-scenes people who keep the horses healthy and in tip-top shape.

THERE ARE NO weekends on the backside and work starts at 4:30 in the morning. There's a whole human aspect to the industry, and that is where the Backside Learning Center comes in.

WE WORK WITH the humans who work with the horses. We connect them with resources.

PART OF MY job is working with kids. I love to organize activities for them or bring in guest speakers, and see their faces light up when they're working on homework and they're struggling, and then it just clicks.

THAT'S A SPECIAL moment.

WILL OLDHAM

MUSICIAN

I DO THINK place is crucial to the extent that the last Bonnie "Prince" Billy record I put out is called *I Made A Place.*

IT'S ALL LOUISVILLE- and Kentucky-based musicians. It's all about Kentucky.

IT'S LIKE, "THIS is it." This is my space.

MY RELATIONSHIP TO country music is fully shaped by this place where we live, and it will be something I continue to decipher until I die, unless I find something better to do.

PEOPLE HAD THESE different preconceptions, misconceptions and stereotypes about Kentucky and its relationship to the South.

MOST PEOPLE ASSUME that it's a part of the South, and we here know that's not a fully accurate description of what we are.

IT DOES APPLY in many ways— some terrible ways, and some halfway decent.

I REMEMBER A review of the first Palace Brothers record that described it as "fiddle-drenched," and there's no violins on it.

YOU UNDERSTAND THEN how much people's perceptions skew reality.

WHEN A SONG succeeds in any way of getting you from point A to another, unknown point, it feels marvelously rewarding.

"I SEE A DARKNESS" has these little lifts and falls that make the song do what we hope a song will do.

ESCORT YOU THROUGH time and emotions so you come out the other side with a transformation or accomplishment or understanding or catharsis.

I WAS OUT in Shelbyville, Kentucky, and I was thinking about friendship.

HOW DO I APPROACH finding a song that could potentially serve a larger purpose?

I WAS TRYING to communicate something to somebody specific, although I never told that person that I was communicating it to them.

IT WAS FOR the audience to hear and potentially share it with people they wanted to say something to.

THROUGHOUT MY musical life, I've sought out collaborations in Australia, Japan, California, Oregon, New York. Now I don't really want to do that.

THOSE THINGS WILL continue to happen, but I think I could spend the rest of my life working in the community here.

STEVEN ALVAREZ

PROFESSOR

I HAD THE opportunity to work at different universities when I was going on the job market after grad school.

....

BUT I WANTED to be somewhere where I studied Mexican people. I went driving around the barrio of Alexandria Drive in Lexington. I went to the Village Branch Library and heard people speaking Spanish, loudly, proudly, not having to be ashamed. I realized there's something special here.

....

THE UNIVERSITY of Kentucky is around 90 percent white. Finding ways to humanize immigrants is not always an easy task, especially when they've been demonized politically.

....

I TOOK THE students on a field trip and we went to Tortillería Y Taquería Ramírez to get them some Mexican food.

....

SOME OF THEM, their exposure was, like, Qdoba, and here there's things on the menu like brains and intestine and tongue, and they're like, "Whoa, what's going on here?"

THE STUDENTS WERE really curious, and then they tried the tortillas. These are tortillas that are made with corn from Weisenberger Mill in Midway. It's Kentucky corn.

....

I REALIZED all the stuff I was trying to do with immigration, language, politics in my classes, we can do through food. That's how Taco Literacy was born at the University of Kentucky.

....

I THINK MOST folks don't think about Latinos in places like Kentucky, but it's one of the fastest growing Latino populations in the country.

....

RIGHT BEFORE the airport, you have to pass through what folks— pejoratively—call "Mexington."

....

NOW THERE ARE a couple generations of Mexican kids and young people who say, "We are 'Mexington.'"

....

"YOU MIGHT'VE BEEN" talking shit about us, but now we're here and we ain't going nowhere."

ROBERT GIPE

WRITER, THEATER PRODUCER

I LIVE IN Harlan County, Kentucky. Coal mining here started around 1911. Since then, that's been the dominant employer. Even as it has become less central to the community economy, it still defines the culture. It's part of almost every family's history.

I GRADUATED COLLEGE without a clear sense of purpose, so I went to graduate school at the University of Massachusetts at Amherst and got a master's in English and American studies. After that, I worked at Appalshop, which is an art center in Whitesburg, Kentucky.

I GOT INVOLVED with the arts and culture of the coalfields. I wasn't thinking about being a writer until we got a grant in 2003 to do community-based artwork and engagement in response to the opioid crisis.

WE DID AN Oxycontin musical.

WE GATHERED ORAL histories and worked with musicians and theater artists. There were a lot of flood stories. We used the metaphor of floods being similar to the flood of prescriptions.

WITH OPIOIDS COMING in, people would be ashamed of becoming addicted. With a flood, we would respond to that collectively. The message of the play was, let's respond to this other flood together.

IT WAS CALLED *Higher Ground*.

AFTER THAT, I saw how storytelling could help people celebrate what they had going for them and use their strengths to address challenges.

WE'VE DONE NINE different *Higher Ground* plays now.

OUR NEIGHBORS DON'T need the community explained, they need it explored. They need to reflect on it.

IN A SPACE of reassurance where we know this community has value.

OUITA MICHEL

CHEF

IN 1987, MY dad helped me pack all my stuff up into a U-Haul trailer.

I HAD TWO friends who debated for Dartmouth who needed a third roommate in Manhattan, so I accepted that challenge and opened up *The New York Times* and got a job in a restaurant.

IT WAS A macrobiotic restaurant.

WHEN I CAME back from New York City, I really became interested in local agriculture in Kentucky.

IT WAS 1993, so everybody felt like there was a war on tobacco. The Burley Tobacco Cooperative in Lexington had started a vegetable cooperative for farmers so that they could start to diversify their crops.

I THINK IT was around that time when I started thinking about the fact that restaurants really need to drive farm revenue—especially small farm revenue—in order to create an economic driver for young people to go into farming.

WHEN WE WERE writing our business plan, we wrote "local agriculture" into the big business plan.

I FEEL THERE is a natural bias against women running systems in our country. I don't think it's unique to the kitchen, by the way.

I DO THINK that when you're the chef of a big restaurant, it's harder to get that position if you are a woman.

SO THAT, IN large part, is why I opened my own restaurant, Holly Hill Inn, in Midway, Kentucky. We've been open for 20 years.

PEOPLE ARE ALWAYS saying, "How's Kentucky's cuisine really unique from other states?" And I'm like, well, there's not too many places you can go to a drive-through and get a bowl of brown beans and cornbread.

YOU CAN STILL do that in Kentucky.

ROB SAMUELS

MAKER'S MARK PRESIDENT

SO MUCH OF the legacy of American whiskey was this frontier whiskey, aggressive and rough.

....

OUR FAMILY HAD made whiskey for 160 years in Kentucky prior to Maker's Mark. At that time, it was like all of the others. You almost had to work hard to like it.

....

MY GRANDPARENTS JUST weren't inspired by it. They wanted to make a bourbon for people who didn't like bourbon.

....

COMING OUT OF Prohibition in the mid-1930s until 1990, guess how many new licensed distilleries in Kentucky were created? There was one. That was us.

....

MY GRANDPARENTS were classmates at university. She graduated first in the class. He graduated not last, but maybe in the bottom third. They resurrected the T.W. Samuels Distillery coming out of Prohibition as newlyweds.

....

THAT WAS THE fifth distillery to reopen in America after Prohibition.

IT WAS commercially viable. It was successful. But they sold it just because they didn't believe in it.

....

MY GRANDFATHER floundered in a couple other businesses. He opened, we believe, the only bank in American history that opened and closed in less than 60 days. Fundamentally, he was not a businessperson.

....

HE WAS a craftsman.

....

MY GRANDMOTHER encouraged him to get back into whiskey, and he said, "I'll get back into whiskey, but it needs to be on my own terms."

....

TO HIM, THAT meant focusing on quality, not quantity.

....

THEY PAID $35,000 in 1952 for hundreds of acres of land. I have the property deed on my desk. I think we are the only distillery in Kentucky that owns its own water source. We have a pipe at the bottom of a spring-fed lake that goes right into the basement of our distillery.

WE'RE A SINGLE source of supply, which means every drop of whiskey that's ever been in one of our bottles, we made, and every drop of whiskey ever made in our distillery has never been anywhere else.

MAKER'S MARK DID not borrow whiskey to get started. They waited almost seven years.

MY GRANDMOTHER CREATED the name, designed the bottle.

SHE CAST THE VISION and designed the entire distillery campus. To our knowledge, Maker's Mark is the only whiskey brand ever named and designed by a woman.

MY GRANDFATHER JUST wanted to name the whiskey after the family, which was customary. She challenged him.

SHE HAD ONE of the most extensive collections of English pewter in the world, and she was really passionate about the craftsmen and women's individual marks.

SHE THOUGHT OF physically hand dipping every bottle in the red sealing wax so each one would be a little special from the next, which is the mark of any handmade piece.

WE HAVE THE very first bottle of Maker's Mark, dated May 8, 1958, and each bottle looks exactly like the very first bottle.

IT'S NEVER CHANGED.

WE STILL HAND cut every label, and we hand dipped 26 million bottles last year.

I SPENT SUMMERS working every job in the distillery: hand dipping bottles on the bottling line, working in the still to the roller mill to the yeast room.

MY FIRST MEMORY walking into the distillery with my grandfather, I was this tall, and he made an impression on me that still carries through everything we do.

HOW IMPORTANT people are.

FRANK X WALKER

POET

I AM ONE of 11, so my childhood was crowded. My first library was a milk crate full of comic books.

WHEN ASKED WHO were the earliest influences on my poetry, I always have to say Stevie Wonder and Marvin Gaye. Curtis Mayfield was my Shakespeare.

MEMBERS OF THE community theater group I helped found had given me the nickname "X" because my eyeglasses looked like the same glasses that Malcolm wore. I had hair then.

A DECADE LATER, I found a lawyer and paid to legally change my name to Frank X Walker.

I WAS AT a reading at the opera house in Lexington in the early '90s. Originally it was subtitled "The Best Writers from Appalachia." Then they invited Nikky Finney and changed the name.

I LEFT, TRYING to reconcile the need to change the name. I looked up *Appalachians* in the dictionary I had at the time. It said, "Appalachians were white people from the mountainous regions of Appalachia."

HAVING TRAVELED through the mountains, having relatives from the same space, knowing that even the official definition of the region included Pittsburgh and Birmingham, I was struck that the word was limited to white people.

I THINK IF I had had a therapist, I'd have just gone to therapy and asked my question. Instead, I just tried to process it on the page.

I WAS TRYING to explore all the things that Black people in that region and white people in that region had in common. Food and porches. The oral tradition and love of music, family.

I WAS PART of a group of writers who met on Monday nights. The very next week I read a poem I'd written about that experience.

THAT VERY NIGHT, we agreed to name ourselves the Affrilachian Poets.

STORIES

_Essays and selected writing by noted
voices exploring the Kentucky landscape_

WENDELL BERRY

Selected Poems

MANIFESTO: THE MAD FARMER LIBERATION FRONT

Love the quick profit, the annual raise,
vacation with pay. Want more
of everything ready-made. Be afraid
to know your neighbors and to die.
And you will have a window in your head.
Not even your future will be a mystery
any more. Your mind will be punched in a card
and shut away in a little drawer.
When they want you to buy something
they will call you. When they want you
to die for profit they will let you know.
So, friends, every day do something
that won't compute. Love the Lord.
Love the world. Work for nothing.
Take all that you have and be poor.
Love someone who does not deserve it.
Denounce the government and embrace
the flag. Hope to live in that free
republic for which it stands.
Give your approval to all you cannot
understand. Praise ignorance, for what man
has not encountered he has not destroyed.
Ask the questions that have no answers.
Invest in the millennium. Plant sequoias.
Say that your main crop is the forest
that you did not plant,
that you will not live to harvest.

Say that the leaves are harvested
when they have rotted into the mold.
Call that profit. Prophesy such returns.
Put your faith in the two inches of humus
that will build under the trees
every thousand years.
Listen to carrion—put your ear
close, and hear the faint chattering
of the songs that are to come.
Expect the end of the world. Laugh.
Laughter is immeasurable. Be joyful
though you have considered all the facts.
So long as women do not go cheap
for power, please women more than men.
Ask yourself: Will this satisfy
a woman satisfied to bear a child?
Will this disturb the sleep
of a woman near to giving birth?
Go with your love to the fields.
Lie easy in the shade. Rest your head
in her lap. Swear allegiance
to what is nighest your thoughts.
As soon as the generals and the politicos
can predict the motions of your mind,
lose it. Leave it as a sign
to mark a false trail, the way
you didn't go. Be like the fox
who makes more tracks than necessary,
some in the wrong direction.
Practice resurrection.

HORSES

When I was a boy here,
traveling the fields for pleasure,
the farms were worked with teams.
As late as then a teamster
was thought an accomplished man,
his art an essential discipline.
A boy learned it by delight
as he learned to use
his body, following the example
of men. The reins of a team
were put into my hands
when I thought the work was play.
And in the corrective gaze
of men now dead I learned
to flesh my will in power
great enough to kill me
should I let it turn.
I learned the other tongue
by which men spoke to beasts
—all its terms and tones.
And by the time I learned,
new ways had changed the time.
The tractors came. The horses
stood in the fields, keepsakes,
grew old, and died. Or were sold
as dogmeat. Our minds received
the revolution of engines, our will
stretched toward the numb endurance
of metal. And that old speech
by which we magnified
our flesh in other flesh
fell dead in our mouths.
The songs of the world died
in our ears as we went within
the uproar of the long syllable
of the motors. Our intent entered
the world as combustion.
Like our travels, our workdays

burned upon the world,
lifting its inwards up
in fire. Veiled in that power
our minds gave up the endless
cycle of growth and decay
and took the unreturning way,
the breathless distance of iron.

But that work, empowered by burning
the world's body, showed us
finally the world's limits
and our own. We had then
the life of a candle, no longer
the ever-returning song
among the grassblades and the leaves.

Did I never forget?
Or did I, after years,
remember? To hear that song
again, though brokenly
in the distances of memory,
is coming home. I came to
a farm, some of it unreachable
by machines, as some of the world
will always be. And so
I came to a team, a pair
of mares—sorrels, with white
tails and manes, beautiful—
to keep my sloping fields.
Going behind them, the reins
tight over their backs as they stepped
their long strides, revived
again on my tongue the cries
of dead men in the living
fields. Now every move
answers what is still.
This work of love rhymes
living and dead. A dance
is what this plodding is.
A song, whatever is said.

A VISION

If we will have the wisdom to survive,
to stand like slow-growing trees
on a ruined place, renewing, enriching it,
if we will make our seasons welcome here,
asking not too much of earth or heaven,
then a long time after we are dead
the lives our lives prepare will live
here, their houses strongly placed
upon the valley sides, fields and gardens
rich in the windows. The river will run
clear, as we will never know it,
and over it, birdsong like a canopy.
On the levels of the hills will be
green meadows, stock bells in noon shade.
On the steeps where greed and ignorance cut down
the old forest, an old forest will stand,
its rich leaf-fall drifting on its roots.
The veins of forgotten springs will have opened.
Families will be singing in the fields.
In their voices they will hear a music
risen out of the ground. They will take
nothing from the ground they will not return,
whatever the grief at parting. Memory,
native to this valley, will spread over it
like a grove, and memory will grow
into legend, legend into song, song
into sacrament. The abundance of this place,
the songs of its people and its birds,
will be health and wisdom and indwelling
light. This is no paradisal dream.
Its hardship is its possibility.

TRAVELING AT HOME

Even in a country you know by heart
it's hard to go the same way twice.
The life of the going changes.
The chances change and make a new way.
Any tree or stone or bird
can be the bud of a new direction. The
natural correction is to make intent
of accident. To get back before dark
is the art of going.

WENDELL BERRY, an essayist, novelist and poet, has been honored with the T. S.
Eliot Prize and the Aiken Taylor Award for poetry, among others. In 2010, he was awarded
the National Humanities Medal by Barack Obama, and in 2016, he was the recipient of
the Ivan Sandrof Lifetime Achievement Award from the National Book Critics Circle.
Wendell lives with his wife, Tanya Berry, on their farm in Henry County, Kentucky.

WALKING ACROSS THE DIVIDE

Written by **HANNAH L. DRAKE** | **SPANNING THE OHIO RIVER** to connect Louisville, Kentucky, to Jeffersonville, Indiana, the Big Four Bridge is a six-span pedestrian and bicycle bridge that has quickly become a symbol of Louisville. Constructed in 1895 as a railroad bridge, it carried freight and passengers between Louisville and Southern Indiana until 1969, when it was decommissioned, its ramps removed several years later. In recent years the bridge was reimagined as a walking bridge, and opened to pedestrians in 2013. At night, it glows in Technicolor lights and shimmers over the water.

A roundtrip walk on the bridge is about 2 miles, and from just about the day of its reopening I looked forward to walking on the bridge almost every day, amazed that I could walk to an entirely different state in just minutes. I would stand on the top of the bridge and look down at the city, take pictures of the sunset, walk into Jeffersonville, Indiana, and get ice cream. I remember taking my niece on the bridge when she was little and watching her skip and run. I saw friends and family members on the bridge. I saw people on bikes, mothers pushing strollers, people in wheelchairs. I recall standing and listening to a young man playing his guitar as I felt the breeze on my face. I remember seeing people in workout clothes trucking up the ramp to the top of the bridge and shouting words of encouragement to them.

The bridge brought us together. The bridge said you belonged here. At the bridge, we could put aside our differences and enjoy moments of being together. The bridge reflected the community. The bridge was the world that I desired to live in.

The bridge has indeed become a symbol of the city, but for me, it represents something so much more because of the story in the water it crosses. My earlier work had brought me to Natchez, Mississippi, where I visited Forks of the Road, the second-largest slave market in the

South. There on the wall, I saw it—a map and hundreds of names and ages of enslaved Black people brought to Mississippi from Louisville, Kentucky, by way of the Ohio River. I was stunned into silence. I had lived in Kentucky for over a decade, and never once did I hear about this history. Here, so far from home, I learned that the river is 1,310 miles long and carries the largest volume of water of any tributary of the Mississippi. The power of the current and Louisville's proximity to the river meant the city became a leading exporter of enslaved people.

Standing on the bridge, I also recalled when I visited Dakar, Senegal. I was with a friend buying earrings. We were so used to Shopping While Black in America that we held the earrings in such a way that the shop owner didn't think we were going to steal them. When we went to pay for them, we realized that the shop owner was speaking to someone outside, not even paying any mind to us inside. It dawned on me: In Senegal, it was not a crime to be Black. And it was as if the entire world opened up to me and said, "Hannah, we have been waiting for you." The moment was so liberating. It was as if I could see the world in color for the first time. It was beautiful.

That feeling of belonging is what I felt at the bridge. I could see Louisville in color, and it was just as vibrant, shining and splendid as those nighttime lights illuminating the Ohio. Then I saw it on social media—a post that a racial slur had been spray-painted on the Big Four Bridge. I was immediately angry. Not this space. Not this space where everyone comes together. Not this space where I believe Louisville got it right. Not this space where everyone is welcomed. I jumped into action and called on people to reclaim the Big Four Bridge by taking a walk with me. How different could this world be if we just took the time to walk together?

Hundreds of people responded to my request, and on a Saturday morning, they came out, and we started out on our Better Than Hate Walk across the bridge. Because that is what a bridge is designed to do. A bridge is designed to connect, not divide. What could this world look like if we built more bridges—not physically, but bridges between people who are different than us? While I understand that Louisville has challenges, we can be better than hate. We have the power to create the spaces that we want to see in the world. We have the ability to create spaces that bring us together and do not pull us apart.

On the day of the Better Than Hate Walk, standing on the bridge,

I saw a world that I believed could exist. As Franz Kafka said, "By believing passionately in something that still does not exist, we create it. The nonexistent is whatever we have not sufficiently desired." What does Louisville desire to be? We get to decide that. We get to decide to create spaces in our city that are inclusive, welcoming, and that say, "You belong here." We get to choose to build bridges between us and then walk on them together. That moment in Dakar when I felt free is what I want to experience all the time in Louisville, and I do at the Big Four Bridge. It reminds me of a world that I do not yet know but that I believe will one day exist.

HANNAH L. DRAKE is an activist, public speaker, poet and author of 11 books. She writes commentary on politics, feminism and race. Hannah was selected by the Muhammad Ali Center to be a Daughter of Greatness, part of a speakers series that features prominent women engaged in social philanthropy, activism and pursuits of justice. Hannah was chosen as one of the Best of the Best in Louisville, Kentucky, for her poem "Spaces" and was recently honored as a Kentucky Colonel, the highest title of honor bestowed by the governor of the state.

YELLOW DIAMONDS IN THE LIGHT

Written by **JASON KYLE HOWARD** | **THERE'S NO GRANDEUR** here, in this squat, two-story building hunched in the heart of downtown Lexington. Next door, the twinkling marquee of the restored Kentucky Theatre juts over the sidewalk, announcing the showtimes of the latest independent films. Tucked in the middle of a nondescript block, even the name itself is bland—The Bar Complex, always shortened [even over the door] to The Bar. Capitalized, The Bar is The One. There are no others. Which isn't quite true, of course. Crossings, a leather bar with well-worn pool tables, is a five-minute walk up the street. A few blocks away, Soundbar, with its preppy college-aged crowd, pulses across from Ole Hookers Bait & Tackle, a lesbian-owned dive offering cheap drinks and nights devoted to karaoke and bingo. But in another way, The Bar's name tells a deeper truth, the kind that lodges in your chest.

It's Saturday night, and every room, every last corner, of The Bar is packed. Enter: navigate the crowd ordering drinks at the long, glossy oak-topped bar on the left, helmed by harried bartenders, and the overflowing row of red-leather banquettes on the right. Follow the din from around the corner and into the next room. Seated at dozens of tables and lining the walls are hundreds of people, drinking and singing and shouting at the queen commanding the stage. Out back, friends huddle and pass a joint. Couples kiss. Back inside and upstairs, another bar and a dance floor, sticky from sloshed liquor and syrupy mixers, the walls lined with mirrors. Everywhere, eyes catch the light and shimmer like the sequined gowns, capes and bodysuits we are watching onstage.

I'm here with my husband, Silas, and another couple, two of our best friends, for the all-too-rare night out. We are in our 30s and 40s and have all aged out of the club scene. Even in my early and mid-20s, spent in Washington, D.C., I never was a barfly. Although I savored the occasional night at clubs—Cobalt, Tracks, Velvet Nation, The Fireplace, JR's—my flirtations usually came via friends-of-friends or in the aisles of a bookshop. Now, as I approach middle age and have settled into a fulfilling marriage, I no longer need to cruise the room. Dinner parties are more our forté. But sometimes you need a night out with your own kind, and for us, a drag show is an enticement—especially when it veers between fierce and tatty, which makes it all the more entertaining.

Each weekend, on Friday and Saturday nights, a procession of queens [along with the occasional king] serve the four elements of drag—charisma, uniqueness, nerve, talent—to varying degrees as they strut, donkey kick, windmill, spin and death drop across the stage of Kentucky's most historically significant gay club. But their moves are not just confined to The Bar. They are taking their glamour out into the city as well, becoming a fixture in restaurants for drag brunches and in libraries for drag queen story hours. It's all part of a marked shift in Lexington. Over the past decade, the city has twice elected a gay mayor and installed permanent rainbow crosswalks, demonstrating the spirit of inclusion and diversity practiced across six decades at The Bar and by the queens themselves.

Kentucky drag, you see, is its own breed. More eclectic than the standard big-city fare, performances venture beyond the usual songs by contemporary divas like Lady Gaga, Rihanna and Ariana Grande. At least one country goddess is guaranteed to make an appearance. Dolly or Shania. Home-state shero Wynonna Judd belting "No One Else on Earth." A queen pulling at the heartstrings with "Strawberry Wine," Deana Carter's plaintive vocals smothered by every last person in the room singing along. Showtunes, or even a gospel standard, and the occasional appearance of a timeless chanteuse. Barbra, Bette, Diana, Liza, Cher. All the while, the costumes swing between glitzy, outrageous ensembles and the more homespun, thrifted variety, while the emcee laces down-home Southern hospitality with a drag show's customary cattiness in a gruff twang.

Tonight: Beyoncé, sleek, shapely and passionate. "Sweet Dreams." Then, Reba, circa 1994—flaming wig teased to the heavens, singing about confronting her inattentive man. Showers of bills and applause for both. Now the mood shifts. The music turns dark, slow, heralding a queen of the old school. My favorite kind.

The black velveteen curtain opens to reveal Judy Garland in all her damaged glory, dolled up in what must be a vintage gown. Beaded, high-necked, well-cut. She belts "The Man That Got Away," a torch song of unrequited love. Judy prowls the stage's perimeter with the occasional pause, extending her left arm in exaggerated choreography to the music's time. Her body is all angles and corners, and along the way she accepts bills and dispenses the occasional air kiss. As the song ramps up in intensity, moving toward its denouement, she returns to center stage for the long, tortured note that comes before the quiet, aching finish. Judy's voice fades to but a whisper, and we are all on our feet as she curtseys and scurries off behind the curtain. There's a brief intermission, and the four of us begin to chat.

I can't seem to shake the melancholy lingering in the air. At first I think it's a holdover from the song, then I realize it's something more. There's a sense of being watched, observed. Not by anyone in the crowd, but from something—a feeling? a ghost?—lurking in the room's shadowy nooks and corners.

The original club on this site opened as a speakeasy in 1939, and while it was not founded as an exclusively gay establishment, the joint nonetheless provided the queer community a discreet place to gather. Twenty-four years later, two gay men purchased the club and christened it The Gilded Cage. It was a dedicated queer space that featured dancing and drag shows, and hosted the likes of Rock Hudson, who was rumored to be one of the bar's financial backers. Through its successive changes in ownership and names—The Living Room in 1967, Johnny Angel in 1978 and, finally, The Bar in the late eighties—what the club provided remained consistent: sanctuary. And not just for LGBTQ+ Lexingtonians, or for queers and queens visiting from other cities. It was then and remains now a haven for rural gays. Tobacco farm boys, sons of coal miners and loggers and mechanics, for those who weren't—who aren't—able to live openly in their communities.

Sometimes, in between drinks or when a queen pays the rare tribute to Judy or Barbra, to Eartha or Miss Ross, I sense those bygone patrons drawing near, hovering. Above the herbal bouquet of gin and the heat of the club, I smell the vetiver and Eau Sauvage and Stetson masking office sweat and mechanic's grease.

City boy, country boy. Did you count down the days to Friday night, Saturday night? All through the week, did you check your watch, longing

for the taste of freedom in a state you may have loved but could not see fit to love you back?

He said it over and over, this 13-year-old kid. But even all these years later, his words still feel like an indictment spoken by the place itself. Queer, queer, queer, queer, he barked from the water, holding on to the edge of the pool, as I stood talking to my friend in the lifeguard chair. The boy's friends laughed, so he kept going, looping the words in steady, staccato rhythm that was finally broken by the dreaded synonym. My friend shot him a withering glance, then she turned back to me, wondering what to do. How to respond. I carried on talking, as if he and his slurs were not even there, unwilling to let him see me break.

A PLACE CAN HAVE A WILL, A HEART, OF ITS OWN. A PLACE IS CAPABLE OF INJURY AND LOVE—AND OF CHANGE.

It was the late '90s, and although I was only 17, I had grown used to such encounters there in southeastern Kentucky, a couple of hours' drive from Lexington, surrounded by mountains and a culture steeped in fundamentalism and machismo. Even in childhood, my body had been policed. Don't sit that way, I was told when I crossed my legs at the knee by instinct. Stand taller, walk straighter, toughen up. And, when I grew attached to a boy in middle school: You need more guy friends. People will get the wrong idea.

There was no place for me here in this conservative state that always seemed to attack my most tender spot, the one I was trying to hide. Where there were realms of masculinity—basketball and football, hunting and fishing, cars and guns—I could never enter. Even as a child I wanted out. At 13, awash in angst and longing, I lip-synched in my bedroom mirror to Barbra Streisand's "Gotta Move," and five years later I did—to Washington, D.C., the city that raised me and most feels like home. It's one of the mysteries of my life: how I ended up here, in Lexington, back in Kentucky. I explain it with practical reasons of occupation, circumstance and timing. But I also now know that home can have more than one meaning: it can be an emotional territory, a landscape located in a gentle set of eyes, in the welcoming crook of an arm, in a good, generous heart.

After the break, more queens. Whitney and Gaga and J.Lo. The gowns and catsuits keep coming, one after the other, a succession of beads and spangles. A bachelorette party orders a round of shots and shoves the bride-to-be up to exchange an appropriate tip for a queenly blessing. Broad-shouldered twentysomethings in clingy shirts line the perimeter of the stage, bouncing their legs to the bass's rhythm as they wait to stuff a five, a ten, a twenty, into the hands of their favorite diva. Then I see her: an older woman, likely in her late 60s, rising from her table in front of center stage to tip the queen. She is beaming while she waits her turn; her face glows as she shuffles to the beat. Every time I come to The Bar I hope she will be here. She's a regular, and I sometimes wonder why, as she is usually alone. Word is that she is straight. I imagine her grandson is one of the performers. Or perhaps there was a brother, a friend, a son she lost—a beloved who found himself, who became himself, in this place. I'm not sure. I have never met her. I can only divine her story.

In 1970, when The Bar was The Living Room, Marjorie Jones and Tracy Knight invited their loved ones to witness their spiritual, if not legal, union after becoming what is thought to be the first lesbian couple in the nation to sue for a marriage license. "What they propose is not a marriage," the courts ruled.

Here, in 1985, Jeffrey Wasson went to the restroom and approached a man he fancied. The undercover officer placed him under arrest, and Wasson fought the charges. Seven years later, the Kentucky Supreme Court ruled in his favor, deciding that the commonwealth guaranteed the right to privacy and equal protection to private, consensual relationships regardless of orientation—11 years before the U.S. Supreme Court would decide *Lawrence v. Texas* along the same lines.

In 2015, 45 years after Jones and Knight were married: marriage equality. Our lesbian cousins wed a block away in the chambers of the judge who had served as Wasson's attorney. Four days later, he married Silas and me in his home, a ceremony witnessed by his own husband and their solemn beagle, by our daughter and son.

I won't pretend. I won't romanticize this place. Outside of Lexington and Louisville, and perhaps a few smaller towns, there's still another Kentucky that is not as hospitable. But here in this city, we take pride in our former mayor and the rainbow crosswalks. And just outside The Bar: a state historical marker honors the club's history, commemorating Jones and Knight's marriage, and Wasson's courage.

A place can have a will, a heart, of its own. A place is capable of injury and love—and of change.

We're upstairs now, the four of us, dancing to the candy-floss lyrics of Melanie C and Sink the Pink's "High Heels." Silas pulls me in for a kiss, and the song transitions into the staccato pulse of Rihanna's "We Found Love." It shoots a jolt of electricity through the room. Across the floor, glasses are raised and drinks spilled; near us, above the beat and lyrics, someone calls out, *My girl!* and he is echoed with shouts of agreement. As we dance, I look around at the mirrored walls, and somewhere, lost in the refraction of all these bodies, I know they are there. We raise our hands, singing along, offering our voices as a testimony, a prayer of thanksgiving, to The Bar and its ghosts. —*For Ernesto Scorsone*

JASON KYLE HOWARD is the author of *A Few Honest Words* and co-author of *Something's Rising*. His work has appeared in *The New York Times*, *Oxford American*, *Salon*, *The Nation*, *The Millions* and in other publications, and on C-SPAN's *Book TV* and NPR. Howard is editor of *Appalachian Review*, a literary quarterly based at Berea College, where he directs the creative writing program, and he serves on the graduate faculty of the Spalding University Sena Jeter Naslund-Karen Mann School of Creative and Professional Writing.

PAPPYLAND
A STORY OF FAMILY, FINE BOURBON, AND THE THINGS THAT LAST

Written by **WRIGHT THOMPSON**
Three chapters excerpted from the 2020 book.

PART I: CHAPTER 1

On the afternoon of the Kentucky Oaks, I searched the grandstand at Churchill Downs for Julian P. Van Winkle III. It was Friday, the day before the Derby, and it looked like it might just stay beautiful and clear, a miracle this time of year in the humid South. As I made my way through a crowd of people with a sheen on their faces and seersucker stuck to their thighs, I thought of an old friend who once said that existing at our latitude felt like living inside someone's mouth. The breath of racehorses, summer humidity, Kentucky Straight Bourbon Whiskey—the South has many forms of heat, byproducts of a place perched delicately on the edge between romance and hypocrisy. The Ole Miss band used to play a slow version of "Dixie" before the game, and even as I winced at the Confederate nostalgia, I also teared up because the song reminded me of my father. That's what Patterson Hood called the "duality of the Southern Thing." The Derby distills those feelings. When horses turn for home, we are all wild and free, sweating and cheering, the dream on our breath and clutched in our fists. I admit I love that bloodsport rush.

The pageant of the big race swirled around me. The old Louisville families gathered in boxes along the stretch, gripping drinks and pari-mutuel tickets. I was at the track to write racing columns for my magazine, and Julian was living another day in what seemed to be the endless spring break of his life. I didn't know him yet. We had met several times before to discuss a book about bourbon we wanted to write together. I was to help him tell the story of his bourbon, the mythical and rare Pappy Van Winkle, but it became clear that there was no way to separate the bourbon's mythology from his personal history. That clarity lay before me. At the moment, I just needed to find the man in the madness at Churchill Downs.

I finally found him holding court in a box about halfway up the grandstand, surrounded by old friends, a well-tailored blue-and-white-striped sport coat draped across his shoulders and reading glasses dangling from his neck beneath a peach-colored, whiskey barrel-patterned bow tie. Julian kept on-brand with his Pappy ball cap, and a lifetime of May afternoons in Kentucky had taught him to put on duck boots before heading to the track. He smiled when he saw me and handed me his flask of Weller 12. The whiskey went down smooth, with enough burn to let you know it was working, which was what my father used to say when he'd disinfect my cuts with hydrogen peroxide. Julian loves the 12-year-old Weller. He's got a storage facility full of it—and a bourbon club's fantasy of other rare bourbons. If you ask him where he keeps it, he'll wink and laugh and dissemble, but he won't give out the coordinates. "I went to the shed," he said. "My whiskey shed, the storage shed, whose location will remain anonymous. I'll show you a picture of it."

His wife, Sissy, saw me and waved. I think I might be in love with her. She's pretty, with a great laugh. Her smile is an invitation to pull up a seat. I had stepped into a party that had been raging for a generation or two. They had a bag of chocolates and a Seven Seas salad dressing bottle filled with bourbon. Julian often travels with his own booze. Wouldn't you? He is famous among friends for showing up at parties with half-pints of Pappy—used for tasting and testing barrels—and passing them around. They're called blue caps. I love the blue caps. Once, before I was about to give a speech, his son, Preston, handed me one to take onstage. I have this memory of Julian at a food and wine festival after-party—it was at a local Indian restaurant that had been turned into a Bollywood dance club—and he was floating around the dance floor, hands in the air, pausing only to give anyone who wanted a pull of the Pappy he kept in his pocket. In that moment, I wanted to know how someone got to be so free and if that freedom created his perfect whiskey, or the other way around. That night exists as a kind of psychedelic dream to me, the feeling of being whisked away in a black Suburban and ending up with streaky images of dancing and music and Pappy.

Julian looks more and more like Pappy every day. He's got a silver cuff of hair around his bald head and is quick with a joke, usually on himself. On his right hand, he wears a family ring just like the one his grandfather and father wore. The Van Winkles have a large number of traditions, the most famous of which is their whiskey. That fame doesn't make it any more or less important than the others. They are all just the things this old Southern family does in the course of being itself. Among Julian's many quirks: wearing fake rotten teeth, which he and Sissy sported each time they first met a set of future in-laws of one of their three daughters; searching for records to fit his old-timey jukebox in the basement;

A LIFETIME OF MAY AFTERNOONS IN KENTUCKY HAD TAUGHT JULIAN TO PUT ON DUCK BOOTS BEFORE HEADING TO THE TRACK. HE SMILED WHEN HE SAW ME AND HANDED ME HIS FLASK OF WELLER 12.

listening to music while cleaning out the big silver pots after frying Thanksgiving turkeys; setting mole traps for going on 40 years now, without ever successfully catching a mole; and firing a paintball gun at the deer on his property that want to tear up his plants. One night, deep into two open bottles of bourbon, he grabbed a flashlight and I grabbed the paintball assault rifle, and we went out into the neighborhood. I kept the weapon up like they do in the war movies, and he swung the light through the trees. We didn't see anything. I was bummed. He was stoic, as usual. Julian almost never complains—few people know, for instance, that he's just on the other side of cancer treatment that could have ended very differently. Normally a private man, he allowed his closest friends to see the fear in his eyes; to share in his vulnerability. His illness made him newly reflective, which would have a cascade of repercussions in his life. He'd reached the point when he had to take dying seriously. Everyone passes through that valley and everyone emerges changed. His bourbon is passing through a valley, too. In the coming months, he will taste the new liquor that will fill his bottles. The whiskey that built his success had run out, and the "new whiskey," distilled and laid up many years ago, is now finally ready to be tasted and, with luck, bottled. I would come to appreciate the challenge of dealing with market trends when your product gets made as many as 25 years in the past. When I met Julian, this is what loomed largest; soon it would be time for him to test the first ever Pappy Van Winkle's Family Reserve made from whiskey distilled by his partner, Buffalo Trace. Whiskey is marketed as an antidote to change, so the magic is especially vulnerable during times of transition. That tension ran through my mind during this otherwise carefree day at the nation's most famous racetrack. Julian was looking far into the future, to see how this brand and whiskey would be passed from one generation to the next. The Van Winkles have done most things very well, except for that: the last time the baton pass got seriously fucked up.

But on this afternoon Julian was in good humor: passing around whiskey, cracking jokes, waiting on the bugle to blow, being Julian Van Winkle. From our box seats, the crowd around us kept an eye on the infield scoreboard, counting down the minutes until post for the next race. People killed time with liquor and stories. A local doctor juggled apples, taking the occasional bite without missing a rotation as we cheered him on.

Finally the next race began with a thunder of hooves. There's a word that describes that sound, *rataplan,* which evokes the incredible noise a dozen running horses can make and the way you feel that noise in your chest, loud—not like something in nature but like standing next to a tower of speakers at an Allman Brothers show. The sound takes on physical form and lives on as psychic echo. The crowd roared and leaned in. We stopped to look down at the track as the horses left the gate and came bounding past. It took less than two minutes, the crowd swaying, clutching the white betting slips, matching numbers to silks, standing and screaming beneath the roof of the grandstand. Oh, glorious afternoon!

Churchill Downs has been expanded over the years, the luxury suites rising high above the spires—an unintentional and dark metaphor about the change that has come to this track. This new-money Derby attracts people who seem desperate for the lifestyle. The day-trippers wear gangster suits and outlandish patterns and hats inappropriate to the latitude, temperature or setting. It's amateur hour. They hold liquor like ninth graders. The homogenization of America has left people wandering the land in search of a place to belong. We are a tribeless nation hungry for tribes. That longing and loneliness are especially on display in early May in Kentucky.

From these seats, it felt possible to ignore all that change. Ignoring can be intoxicating. The view before us was the view people saw one hundred years ago. We couldn't make out the big battleship bridge behind us that dwarfed the spires. We only saw the flash of the silks and the splashes of dirt and the blur of whip hands banging away for one more burst of speed. The race ended, and Julian pulled a Cohiba out of his pocket and lit it. "My victory cigar," he said. A grin flashed across his face. "I didn't bet on the race," he said. "So I won."

PART II: CHAPTER 18

This is where Julian was working when he got the call that would change his life. This is where he started to become sort of cultural icon. He remembers the phone call perfectly. It was from a woman named Patty. She worked at what is now Diageo and called to tell Julian that they had excess whiskey for sale. The company was unloading its bourbon: from shutting down the Stitzel-Weller plant to shedding its famous brands to trying to find buyers for the barrels in its warehouses. The big corporation didn't know what it had; it got rid of the old machines and Pappy's living yeast. Bourbon was part of its past, and so these barrels needed to go. They were priced as low as $200 each. For an entire barrel. Julian flipped page after page and wondered why an enormous corporation with lawyers and accountants and vice presidents and meetings and conference calls didn't see the same value he saw on those pages. Until then, Julian had been buying barrels from the Old Boone distillery and bottling that as Old Rip Van Winkle. Every now and then he'd get some barrels of Stitzel-Weller and put them out under a special label, including the best whiskey I've ever personally tasted, sitting at his kitchen island, a 1968 distillation that was bottled as Family Reserve in 1984. Bourbon heads will recognize the label as being nearly similar to the one he uses now for the Van Winkle rye.

Patty needed to move product. In hindsight, United Distillers took a huge bank vault of money and lit it on fire. The truth is, nobody understood what they had given up and what, in those thousands of barrels they were using as part of the Crown Royal blend, they still had. But Julian did. That was the taste of his youth, and the last pieces he could hold of his father and grandfather. Fine, aged wheated bourbon was his family's legacy—that's what he was really trying to protect. "Of course I believed in it because it was really good," he said. "That's when I got excited, because I tasted that whiskey. I was bottling Old Boone and all this other shit. I tasted the Stitzel-Weller stuff that Master Distiller Ed Foote was making since we sold the distillery and it was awesome."

Looking at this list of barrels, he knew what he needed to do. Each barrel, depending on evaporation, was good for 10 to 18 cases of whiskey. He called a local banker looking for a loan, offering the stock he'd inherited from his father as collateral. The first banker refused, saying these barrels weren't worth the money they'd have to loan Julian to buy them. Finally, after making his case, he got someone to extend him a line of credit and he began buying up as many barrels as he could afford. In the bottling of it, he felt he should pay respect to his family and to the distillery that made this beautiful whiskey, so he named his brand Van Winkle Family Reserve and put Pappy's picture on the label. "The first year we bottled the 20-year-old it was awesome," Julian said, "and I was like making eggnog with 20-year-old Pappy. I felt really guilty but boy it was really good eggnog. I had cases of this stuff sitting around and it was so good. I couldn't believe how good it was, because this was 20-year-old Stitzel-Weller bourbon not stored on a top floor, but the cooler floors. We don't have anything like that anymore because it's gone."

That's how it happened. He survived. Being in Lawrenceburg with Julian is so powerful and hard to explain, because his relief at his survival pours off him. His father ran out of time, same as mine, but this place is where Julian made his own time. He'd held on long enough for someone to come looking for a man who always makes fine bourbon, at a profit if he can, at a loss if he must ... but always fine bourbon.

Pappy came out and got a perfect 99-score review from the Beverage Testing Institute in 1996, which named it the greatest bourbon in the world. Here's one last bit of myth busting: although Julian created Pappy as a vehicle for that Stitzel-Weller, a bourbon bottler never ever wastes juice, so the liquor in that famous bottle rated a 99 wasn't the Stitzel-Weller but some of the Old Boone that was left over. He needed to finish up the last of that before getting to the truly transcendent stuff. So Julian is one of the few people who knows that Pappy got that first 99 and then the really great whiskey started to come out in the bottles bearing the picture of his granddad. Julian stayed out in the wilderness until he made a bourbon that caught the public's imagination, and six years and dozens of barrels of Stitzel-Weller later, Buffalo Trace called and offered to buy into his brand and Julian left Lawrenceburg forever. His success made me think about my dad, and his dad, who both ran out of time, and about Julian, who'd endured—who made his own time—and found through his work and struggle the life-giving forces that eluded his father. He made the trip. He made it for both of them.

PART II: CHAPTER 19

People don't treat Julian like a celebrity. I've been around celebrities. There's a different kind of respect for him. Supplicants want an audience more than proof of life. He doesn't inspire selfies as much as handshakes. We sat courtside at a University of Kentucky basketball game, directly behind Coach Cal, who screamed at his players during one tense time-out, "This isn't high school!" As Julian and I peered around the assistants to follow the action, a man walked over and gathered his nerve and said, tentatively, "Mr. Van Winkle?"

Julian smiled and took the man's hand.

"I'm a big fan of your bourbon," the man said and then excused himself, having delivered the message that pulled him from his seat and sent him down past the scorer's table to the Kentucky bench. A few minutes later, Julian saw a woman he knew in the stands with her new baby and after he waved big, he leaned over to me, grinned, and said, "Future customer."

This is the life that started for him after Pappy. "The cult bourbon shit," Julian called it. I've seen the madness up close, again and again. Not long after our day in Lawrenceburg, Julian, Preston, and I went out to San Francisco for WhiskyFest. We stood behind their table and waited for the hordes to descend. Every age of Pappy was on the table in front of us, and then the doors opened and the line wound around the whole hotel ballroom. Someone wanted the 24-year-old, which doesn't exist. Julian chuckled and said, "We've got 23, 20 and 15."

"You're saving the 24-year-old for yourself," the guy said.

People lined up and got a small pour of whiskey and a photo and a few words. The first bottle of 23-year-old was gone in six minutes. I was counting. Someone asked for the empty bottle. Preston politely told him no and, when nobody was looking, scratched the label so people couldn't sell it online full of cheap whiskey. Eight minutes later, the second and final bottle of 23-year-old was gone. People would be lined up for hours. A few liquor store owners got aggressive with Julian and Preston about how much they were sent every year. "How is it I spend so much money, and I don't have enough allocation?" a man asked. "How do I get more allocation?"

That is the question that follows the Van Winkles around the bourbon world, and nobody wants to hear the real answer: they have no say over who gets their

PEOPLE DON'T TREAT JULIAN LIKE A CELEBRITY. THERE'S A DIFFERENT KIND OF RESPECT FOR HIM. HE DOESN'T INSPIRE SELFIES AS MUCH AS HANDSHAKES.

whiskey or over how much retailers charge for it. Julian is forever raging about how the state liquor boards control the allocations. In New York, for instance, he can't even make sure that Eleven Madison Park, a Michelin-starred restaurant that has supported his whiskey since before it was cool, gets as much as it wants. The whole thing feels corrupt. Ed is always checking price tags and complaining to store owners about their outrageous markups. Once he ordered Pappy at a bar near a ski resort and what they poured out of the bottle was not Pappy. They told him he was wrong. He asked to see the manager. The manager asked how he could tell. Ed explained his connection. The manager said he'd check and never returned. The next day, the bottles were gone.

Sometimes shit happens at the plant. A few years ago, a bunch of whiskey went missing from the distillery itself. The local papers called it Pappygate. A loading dock employee stole around $100,000 of whiskey that he worked to sell through a syndicate made up of members of his rec-league softball team. The bottle scam feels like the kind of small detail that could serve as the opening metaphor in a book about the fall of the American republic. This ham-fisted minor-league Cornbread Mafia also trafficked in guns and steroids.

A law enforcement whiskey enthusiast stopped by the table in San Francisco. Everywhere Julian went, people wanted to talk about the stolen whiskey.

"Do you mind me asking," the cop said, "I recently read that with the recent convictions with everyone that's pled with the bourbon heist, how did that affect your company and how things are going?"

Julian smiled thinly. "We were selling everything we had before the robbery, and we're selling everything we have after the robbery," he said. "So all it did was make the supplies that much tighter and now people hear about us because of the robbery and they want to get some of the whiskey, and it makes it even harder to find, so it makes things worse for you all."

As I took in the event, I realized I'm seeing the same scene playing out over and over again. Some people were real asshats. The whole thing caused a visceral reaction that caught me off guard. It didn't make sense or even reflect the overall spirit of the event. Most people were lovely and sharing a bucket-list experience with friends, and yet I hated to admit that the longer I stood here, the more I focused on the asshats. It was strange and exhausting. An idea floated around my subconscious, stubbornly refusing to cohere enough to acquire the power of language, but there was some chain of unintended consequences going on here to create both this event and my reaction to it. Bourbon became popular again, and then it became expensive and rare, which made it more popular and yet so hard to get that its original purpose as a way to facilitate and lubricate fellowship was being replaced by the hunting for and finding of it. The economy of bourbon was pushing out what I loved most about it. Maybe that's why I was reacting so strongly. When the event finally ended, Julian and Preston looked wiped out. They both needed a drink.

"Where you wanna go?" I asked.

"Someplace nearby," Julian said. "Somewhere with good vodka. I'm getting tired of all this whiskey."

We both laughed. It was time to fade into the night and for me to consider what all I'd seen.

I'd always thought that bourbon was a tool. At WhiskyFest it felt like something people wanted to possess. That was weird to me. You drink expensive bourbon and then you piss it out. No getting around that. It's just passing through. While it's in your system, if you don't drink too much of it and try to start a fight or some shit, that's where the brief, flickering magic happens. Whiskey warms your insides and not just literally. There didn't seem like a lot of warming going on in San Francisco, just a pelt-hunting mad dash.

One night at the Van Winkles' house, I got on my high horse about how ridiculous I found the fetishizing of whiskey, the way it is turned into the event itself as opposed to either a lubricant for the event or a way to shine a light on the unspoken meaning of an event. I was trashing the festivalgoers and both Julian and Sissy politely scolded me. People should be able to express their passion for something they love in whatever way they want, and the communities brought together by people who drink and discuss whiskey were no less valid than those where people drink whiskey and discuss baseball or politics or military history. I was being a snob and imposing my own values and biases onto other people. If they'd learned anything touring the world serving Pappy—Sissy worked those first events with Julian, before anyone had ever heard of them or wanted to buy a bottle—it was the knowledge that there were always a few jackasses but that they were usually outshone by the people who came to meet them, and to try a taste, with an earnest intention, with real pureness of heart.

They've seen a tribe spring up around their whiskey, seen many tribes, really: those who buy it as a status symbol, those who can't find it and long for it, those who can't find it and blame everyone and especially them for that inability. It was an odd and beautiful thing to behold, more like seeing the northern lights than a strong brand culture. To explain, Sissy told me a story about a whiskey festival in New York years ago.

There was this guy, a doctor, a small, gentle man who had brought his father and friends to WhiskyFest. They really hit it off, laughing, as he got to the front of the line. His name was Elliot Goldofsky. Then, later, she ran into him again, with all his friends, and as he introduced her, they told her he was the best otolaryngologist in America. She asked what on earth that meant. Everyone laughed. Sissy and Elliot got to talking, first about surface things like bourbon, and then later about really important things like life. At one point he blurted, "I feel so strongly we were meant to meet this evening."

She went home. A week later, she and Julian found out their young son, Preston, was partially deaf. Now, four decades later, sitting at their dinner table in Kentucky, she began to cry. She cried then, too, she said, and went back into the story. They'd exchanged information and she found his number and called up to New York. Her voice broke when he answered.

"Elliot," she said. "I need you."

She smiled at me. Tears were still in her eyes. Elliot helped them choose the doctor who operated on Preston to try to restore his hearing. Now Preston will be the one to carry on those traditions and share them with people like a random doctor who came out to get a drink with some friends.

WRIGHT THOMPSON is a senior writer for ESPN and the bestselling author of *The Cost of These Dreams*. He lives in Oxford, Mississippi, with his family.

DIRECTORY & INDEX

DIRECTORY

DISTILLERIES

Angel's Envy *Louisville*

Bardstown Bourbon Company *Bardstown*

Barrel House Distilling Co. *Lexington*

Barton 1792 Distillery *Bardstown*

Bluegrass Distillers *Lexington*

Boone County Distilling Co. *Boone County*

Boundary Oak Distillery *Radcliffe*

Brough Brothers Distillery *Louisville*

Buffalo Trace Distillery *Frankfort*

Bulleit Distilling Co. *Shelbyville*

Casey Jones Distillery *Hopkinsville*

Castle & Key Distillery *Frankfort*

Copper & Kings *Louisville*

Evan Williams *Louisville*

Four Roses Distillery *Lawrenceburg*

Green River Distilling Co. *Owensboro*

Hartfield & Co. *Paris*

Heaven Hill *Bardstown*

James E. Pepper *Lexington*

Jeptha Creed Distillery *Shelbyville*

Jim Beam American Stillhouse *Clermont*

Kentucky Artisan Distillery *Crestwood*

Kentucky Peerless Distilling Co. *Louisville*

Limestone Branch Distillery *Lebanon*

Lux Row Distillers *Bardstown*

Maker's Mark Distillery *Loretto*

MB Roland Distillery *Pembroke*

Michter's Fort Nelson Distillery *Louisville*

New Riff Distilling *Newport*

Old Forester Distilling Co. *Louisville*

Old Pogue Distillery *Maysville*

Preservation Distillery *Bardstown*

Rabbit Hole Distillery *Louisville*

Second Sight Spirits *Ludlow*

Stitzel-Weller Distillery *Shively*

Three Boys Farm Distillery *Frankfort*

Three Keys Distillery *Burlington*

Town Branch Distillery *Lexington*

Wild Turkey Distillery *Lawrenceburg*

Wilderness Trail Distillery *Danville*

Willett Distillery *Bardstown*

Woodford Reserve Distillery *Versailles*

BOURBON BARS

Amsden Bourbon Bar *Versailles*

Barn8 *Goshen*

Bluegrass Tavern *Lexington*

Bourbon Haus 1841 *Covington*

Bourbon on Main *Frankfort*

Bourbon on Rye *Lexington*

The Brown Hotel Lobby Bar *Louisville*

Doc Crow's Bourbon Room *Louisville*

Merrick Inn *Lexington*

meta *Louisville*

ONA *Lexington*

Prohibition Bourbon Bar *Newport*

Proof on Main *Louisville*

Talbott Tavern *Bardstown*

The Silver Dollar *Louisville*

Trouble Bar *Lonsville*

Whiskey Bear *Lexington*

Wiseguy Lounge *Covington*

Brandy Library *Manhattan, NY*

Barrel Proof *New Orleans, LA*

Liberty Bar *Seattle, WA*

Longman & Eagle *Chicago, IL*

Nickel City *Austin, TX*

The Old Gold *Portland, OR*

The Patterson House *Nashville, TN*

Raised by Wolves *San Diego, CA*

The Sugar House *Detroit, MI*

LIQUOR SHOPS

The Blind Pig Bourbon Market *Bardstown*

Justins' House of Bourbon *Lexington*

Old Town Wine and Spirits *Louisville*

Morris Deli *Louisville*

Red Dot Liquor *Frankfort*

Revival Vintage Bottle Shop *Covington*

Toddy's Liquors *Bardstown*

Westport Whiskey & Wine *Louisville*

Astor Wine & Spirits *Manhattan, NY*

The Austin Shaker *Austin, TX*

France 44 Wine & Spirits *Minneapolis, MN*

Moreno's Liquors *Chicago, IL*

Woodland Wine Merchant *Nashville, TN*

INDEX